BLUE ROOM

BLUE ROOM

Beverley Hutton

King's Pen

BLUE ROOM

Published by King's Pen
An imprint of Spiderwize

Spiderwize
Office 404, 4th Floor
Albany House
324/326 Regent Street
London
W1B 3HH
UK

www.spiderwize.co.uk

Cover image by Will Gibson www.flickr.com/photos/wigiphotography/

ISBN: 978-0-9568797-0-7

"This story is a very relevant one today and needs to be told. Beverley is a walking miracle and to witness her maturity and poise today gives hope to others struggling to come to terms with a dysfunctional past. I have been privileged to watch the healing and development in Beverley's life that leads me to be able to recommend her story to you so unequivocally..." Rev Jonathan Wilmot, Greyfriars Church, Reading

'This book gives a contemporary reminder of God's ancient power to heal physically, mentally and spiritually. As a doctor in general practice it can be difficult to gain insight into some conditions that rarely present in a straightforward manner and I therefore feel that this book will be a valuable resource to all those working in the medical professions...' Dr M Davies

"Beverley's experience of finding recovery through a faith in Christ is a moving one. I found this book a very interesting and unusual experience and I am sure that many sufferers may well find it helpful. Beverley describes her illness very openly and I am sure that sufferers will be able to relate to the experiences she talks about...." Dr K Tchanturia, Institute of Psychiatry

"This book was so deeply moving and so honestly shared it really must be shared with others. It not only gives hope but it demonstrates the depth and power of God's love and deliverance that is available to all. I want others to receive the blessings we received and the sense we had touched something very sacred and special..." R Patterson

'This is very likely to be the most important and helpful book for Christian people with eating disorders ever to go into print...' Rev Pads Dolphin, St Matthews Church, Southcote

For Paul, Nicholas and Jonathon,
with all my love

"The Lord saved me from death; he stopped my tears and kept me from defeat. And so I walk in the presence of the Lord in the world of the living. I kept on believing, even when I said, 'I am completely crushed,' even when I was afraid and said, 'No-one can be trusted.'

What can I offer the Lord for all his goodness to me? I will bring a wine-offering to the Lord to thank him for saving me. In the assembly of all his people I will give him what I have promised."

Psalm 116: 8-14

Table of Contents

Foreword

I first met Beverley when we both attended a conference entitled 'Helping Others Find Freedom in Christ'. On that occasion she shared with me something of her story, which involved a long struggle with anorexia nervosa. She told me how she had been miraculously healed in 1987, and had subsequently learnt to renew her mind through the teachings of Freedom in Christ Ministries. She was at that time working on a book about her experiences and asked me if I would take a look at her manuscript.

Out of this original contact a friendship was formed. As I was interested in Freedom in Christ Ministries for family reasons, and was working on a book of my own, we soon found there was quite a lot of common ground. As a result I was eventually asked to put together a collection of personal stories from folk whose lives had been turned around by this teaching. This book was later published under the title 'Songs of Freedom'.

When I started to read Beverley's story, I was moved, and at times deeply disturbed by what she had written. I felt at once that it was a story which should certainly be made public.

Now, several years later, Beverley's book is available. It will, I believe, be a blessing to all who read it, as it traces the painful journey of one woman's passage through the valley of the shadow of death – a painful, though ultimately triumphant pathway to healing and joy.

The late Joanie Yoder, author of 'The God Dependent Life', and founder of Yeldall Manor, made the following commendation when she first read Beverley's story:

'It is extremely rare, sad to say, that someone with a long, severe history of anorexia nervosa is still alive, much less free of this horrific disorder. Beverley Hutton is one of those rare people.

However, the longer I know Beverley, the more convinced I become that she needn't remain such a rarity. The media has been making us all aware of the growing number of people who are suffering and dying from this life-dominating illness. Beverley longs to offer them the spiritual help and hope that finally liberated her, and to do so in the form of an autobiographical book. Along with numerous other people who know her as a dedicated wife, mother and Christian, I wholeheartedly support Beverley in her efforts to write her story.

I believe that such a book would do far more than help the sufferers themselves; it also would enlighten surrounding family members and carers, as well as clergy and church workers, through the insights of one who has been there and is alive and well to tell the story. I therefore highly recommend her story. It could, and doubtless would, save other lives.'

As one who has been asked to write a foreword for Beverley's book, I too would warmly recommend it.

Eileen Mitson

Eileen is the author of several books, her most recent being Pathways to Joy, *published by Eagle, and* Songs of Freedom, *published by Monarch*

Chapter 1

"I Want My Mummy!"

AS I STARED at my computer screen the words began to fade into a blur of jumbled meaningless patterns. The usual drone of chatter, of printers spewing out paper, of telephones ringing incessantly, of managers chasing results, all fell away. The office and all its paraphernalia receded into some far-flung shadowy world as memories burst onto the forefront of my consciousness. My eyes glistened with the first tear.

♣

With the wind rushing past my face and my hair flying out behind me, momentarily everything seemed familiar again. Deep in thought I let the swing come slowly to a standstill. As I looked down at the buttons on my knitted blue dress I was aware of a sense of déjà vu which, whilst it intrigued me, was also unnerving. Sometimes it felt as if I was living in a dream, like nothing was real anymore. I sensed an emptiness and an aching inside myself, a desperate sense of unease. I was only seven and I didn't understand what any of this meant.

I hopped off the swing to wander down the path at the side of the house with no particular objective in mind. Orange-blossom overhanging the path filled the air with its sweet, heady aroma. Always being in the shade and home to the dustbin meant the path was dank with other more unpleasant smells at times. It reminded me of the nightmares I suffered night after night: never-ending cycles of revolving images and feelings that switched from light to dark; from delicate white flowers to thick oppressive leather. The contrast made me sick.

Later that night as I lay precariously close to slipping and giving myself away, I peered through the banisters into the deathly silent room below. The weekly group of people had gathered as usual in our lounge and I tried desperately hard to catch even the odd word that would give me some indication as to what was going on. Some of the faces I recognised but others were strangers. A black bearded man with piercing blue eyes made me feel particularly uneasy. There was something strangely sinister about him and as his eyes caught mine and held them, I froze.

As I lay in my bed, troubled and restless, my thoughts turned to my younger sister, Louisa. Anger and jealousy began to surface as I wondered how it was possible that she could be so apparently content when I was not. I felt different. I had to live my life putting on a front because if they knew how I really felt, if they knew the real me, then I would be loved less, I was sure. Louisa was blonde, petite with elfin-like features whilst I was dark and well built. I was intensely jealous, so making the situation worse by confessing my fear and loneliness was not worth contemplating. I was so scared; so very scared of what mum and dad were doing but even more scared of telling them because I knew how important it was to them.

♣

I fled the room, determined to get out of the hospital. Rob, one of the patients, was standing in front of the fire escape. "Open it! Open it! Quick! Let me out!" Rob fumbled with the bar, but all the doors had been locked since I had last run up the corridor. Hanging onto his jumper, I pleaded with him, crying, "Help me!"

Within moments we were surrounded by male nurses and as they tried to prise my fingers from Rob's jumper, I slid to the floor. Grabbing hold of his legs I kicked out, screaming at them, before trying to scrabble away, more as if I was about to become the victim of a violent crime. A scene in a film flashed through my mind afterwards as I thought about Rasputin being stabbed to death by three male nurses as he frantically and hopelessly crawled across the floor to escape. A sea of dazed faces watching on from a distance faded into the background, each seemingly unaware of the horror I was enduring as our paths briefly touched at different moments in each of our troubled lives.

Ian, Steve and Tom fought to get hold of me and it was all over — I hadn't the strength against the three of them. Tom and Ian held my arms whilst Steve picked me up by my legs and they started to carry me back to the empty room as I continued to lash out at them. It wouldn't have made any difference but was a demonstration of the little control I had left. I bit Tom's arm as he held onto me, screaming obscenities at them, to which Steve simply replied, "Go on!

Scream louder if you want! In fact you can have hysterics all day for all I care, but it won't do you any good because you're going back in that room whether you like it or not." They threw me down onto the bed as I screamed, sobbing, "I hate you, all of you!" They turned, laughing, and walked away.

Images of the hospital bed in that dismal stark room, where I was imprisoned from life outside, began to fade.

♣

I woke with a start. The atmosphere in the room was icy. Before there was time to contemplate the cold, a brute force pushed me down into the bed as I felt wave upon wave of sheer evil surging through me. I gasped for breath on every penetration, feeling like I was going to suffocate from the intensity of the assault. What was happening to me? Was I going to die? I tried to see who was there but the room was empty. Nobody was there. But I could *feel* him, the pain tearing through every part of my body, and mind.

Each stabbing thrust seemed an age apart, enough time for me to wonder whether it was over. But it wasn't over. On and on it persisted savaging my body, and with every pulse I wondered if I would survive.

Please don't let the children come in and see this, I prayed as I fought to breathe.

"Mummy! Mummy! Help me!" A little voice cried out from somewhere deep inside my mind, but went unanswered.

The bed stilled. Silence filled the room. Had he really gone? I lay still. I could hear life continuing on as before downstairs. I could hear the television and Paul calling the boys. I wanted to scream but I lay in silence.

"Mummy! I want my mummy!" I curled up in a ball on the bed and as the bedroom and the world faded away all I could hear was the little girl continuing to cry out for her mummy. Desperate cries to be rescued reverberated around the room through every part of my mind. But nobody came.

♣

The room was in semi-darkness when I went in.   A foreboding heaviness lingered in the air. I felt a strange sense of disquiet, mixed with inquisitiveness. I was fourteen and had asked numerous questions about the goings on in the blue room, needing to feel included in whatever it was that was so important, so precious to them.   Every Monday Louisa and I had to stay in our rooms, knowing instinctively to be quiet. We didn't even talk to each other but remained in seclusion in our own bedrooms. We'd never made a noise or been shouted at for disturbing them: there was a sense of something so mysterious about the blue room, something that terrified us so much that we weren't able to confide in each other for fear of making it more real.

'Christos' was a form of regression through which you relived past lives. The group had been experimenting with Christos for some time by then and as I lay down on the settee surrounded by the group of adults, one of them clenched her hand into a fist, rubbing my forehead in a circular motion as she explained that this was the position of the third eye. Another massaged my feet. Both of these points were believed to be the exit points for the soul. Looking up towards the ceiling I became aware of three shadowy black beings staring back down at me.

Dad was to be my point of reference between the physical and spiritual world. He would guide me by asking questions and I was to report back everything to him as it happened. Therefore it was dad who suggested to me that it was time to leave my body and to move towards those dark beings. As I allowed my mind to follow his words, I became aware of being able to look down on my body from the ceiling as if it was somebody else lying there, after which the sky seemed to open up before me and I was flying. The land spread out before me as if in an invisible helicopter surrounded by bright blue sky. I would have been happy to continue flying but dad was directing me to land.

As I started the descent I was aware of a mass of quizzical black faces staring up at me. Flying through the air had felt entirely natural in this situation but the silence below made me uneasy. I landed amongst the huge crowd whilst dad was asking me to tell him who I was. It felt awkward at first to talk to him surrounded by this unknown audience, but as I looked down at myself the rest of my surroundings faded and I saw that I was wearing a long gown and was able to report back that my name was Mary.

"What's happening? Where are you?" dad questioned before asking me to move on in time. I was standing by a quayside looking out to sea and was crying bitterly. "Why are you crying?" dad was enquiring in his subdued monotone.

"He's leaving me!" I sobbed.

I couldn't stop crying, couldn't rid myself of the intense grief, my own grief, despite the fact that dad was trying to get me to move on in time. When I remained caught up in that moment they brought the session to a close, but the room remained in semi-darkness and the group continued in meditation.

Nobody communicated, the room was silent.   Almost immediately after I closed my eyes again, a leather-clad hand reached from behind and grabbed me around my mouth, yanking my head back.   With sheer terror I saw the guillotine above me moments before it dropped and severed my legs from the remainder of my body.   Letting out an almighty scream I couldn't hold back... the guillotine faded as if never there and the entire room turned to stare at me as I looked down at my legs to see that they were still attached.

As I lay on my bed that night unable to sleep for thinking about what had happened, I tied to focus my eyes on familiar objects in my room. I realized that I couldn't see them properly because obscuring my perception was a transparent world overlapping mine, with walls, angles and corners that didn't belong there. I became increasingly alarmed as I began to feel I wasn't a part of anything real any more. I was slipping in and out of an osmotic world, unable to tell what was real and what wasn't. Finally I heard a voice scream from within the silence. "Dad!" It was me screaming, trying to muster all the energy I could to find a voice in this strange void.

"It sounds as if we didn't finish the Christos off properly," he explained, without any hint of alarm. He drew a circle of salt around me on the bed, encouraging me to perform 'exercises' that were supposed to draw my soul back into my body, explaining that my soul had been left half in my body and half out. Eventually I drifted off into a restless sleep.

♣

"Mummy! Help me!" I curled up in a ball as my childhood bedroom faded away. "Mummy! Mummy!" I was annoyed with that little girl.

"Will you shut up!" I answered curtly. "There's no point calling for her because she never comes anyway."

"I want my mummy!" the voice cried endlessly nevertheless, until I drifted back into sleep.

Then I was dreaming. I was only little and I was being held down by things I couldn't see. I knew what was about to happen and I knew it was going to hurt. I began to cry. I screamed for my mummy but she didn't come.

"It's okay, it's only a dream!" Paul was saying as I lashed out, kicking and muttering incoherently. I finally awoke as I heard myself scream "Mummy!" As I lay there in the darkness of our bedroom, suddenly aware of Paul beside me and the realisation that he had woken me from another nightmare, I also became aware that I recognised the voice I kept hearing crying for mummy. It was the same voice in the dream. It was me when I had been a little girl. With the realisation came peace. Peace flooded through me and I felt safe to go back to sleep. The little girl had been me all along.

♣

We moved house several times as dad's business became more successful. He was an exhibition organiser and had his own factory where the exhibition stands were designed and constructed. Lyndhurst Lodge was so big that we couldn't even fill it all to start with and a couple of rooms were left completely unfurnished with just bare boards. In fact one room remained empty for the whole time we lived there, but we still moved to a bigger house eighteen months later to better accommodate my grandparents who came to live with us.

Coming through the front door at Lyndhurst Lodge, you were welcomed into a huge reception hall facing a large staircase which ascended between three wooden pillars supporting two arches. The stairs turned at right angles as they ascended three storeys and you could look down to the bottom from what seemed to me an amazing and somewhat daunting height from the third floor.

My bedroom took up most of the top floor with the other bedrooms on the second. Mine was such an enormous bright sunny room, made all the more so by the fact that dad and granddad had painted the walls in lemon yellow at my request. I had a pretty leaded-light window looking out from under the eaves across the roof of next door and down the quiet lane running round the corner. It seemed so high up and my bed seemed lost in the expanse of space I had up there. In fact were it not for the constant fear I sensed in that house it would have been the envy of any child.

Louisa and I made a thrilling discovery one day as we explored the roof space beyond the back of an under-eaves cupboard in my room. Shining a torch across the rafters, its beam came to rest on the entrance to a small, dark and foreboding passageway. We resolved not to venture further into the black space until we had reinforcements. And so it was with great excitement and nervousness that we enlisted some friends from next door to help us explore whatever lay beyond.

"Are you sure it's safe?" someone whispered as we crawled gingerly along the beams on our hands and knees with only one Christmas cracker torch between us and the fear of spiders brushing through our hair. I had visions of falling through the roof onto the drive below. Or worse, just a leg going through and dad being furious.

"Come on, scaredy-cat, you've got to come too!" I insisted, as Louisa hesitated. Fear hung in the air with each one of us as jumpy as the other. With the hair prickling on the back of my neck I squeezed myself into the triangular hole and began to edge myself further along the roof beams.

"Can you see anything yet?" one of them whispered from behind.

"There's an opening up ahead but it's all dark. I can't see anything yet," I whispered back in a voice equally as shaky as the other.

"Do you think we'll get stuck?" someone helpfully added further back behind me.

Slowly and awkwardly we continued the crawl into cobwebbed pitch blackness, save for the small beam of light up front.

As I emerged from the restricted passageway I was amazed to discover that I could stand up. Swinging the torch wildly from side to side to cover as much of the area as I could for fear of missing anything that might be lurking there, we were momentarily struck dumb to find that the passageway opened up into a large room. It appeared to be completely empty. In total silence each stood, trying to take it in and understand why it was there in the first place. Whilst the moment seemed to last a lifetime, within a matter of minutes each one of us had come to the same decision — escape!

"I'm going back!" someone dared to stutter first, followed by a frenzied few seconds as everybody made a dash for the passage at once and the safety of the cupboard beyond, with no-one wanting to be last.

It was then that I realised that the toy cupboard in my room had in fact once been a passage into the secret room. It had been boarded up when the house had been converted and modernised immediately prior to our purchase of it. Ten years old and alone at night on the third floor in this huge room, I often lay awake too afraid to shut my eyes. What might be in the secret room that the torch beam had missed that would come crawling down the passageway once I closed my eyes?

♣

The door opened and Paul walked in. Tears prickled my eyes as he sat down beside me. "Hold me, please..." I whispered. And as he put his arms around me, the tears began to fall as I held on to him for dear life. "I've just been raped!" I sobbed, "And I don't know who it was. I could feel him but I couldn't see anyone! I don't know if it was a memory or if it's just happened!"

"Did it feel like a memory?" Paul asked, remaining calm whilst inside he felt some sort of sick dread in the pit of his stomach. Yet another crisis, like all the others over the years. Why can't life be normal, he thought, not so unreasonably?

"It felt like it was happening but it couldn't have, could it?" The possibility that it hadn't just happened raised more questions than if it had. If it was a memory, then who had done it in the past, and why didn't I remember? It didn't make any sense.

♣

As I played the piano in one of the large otherwise empty rooms, I paused momentarily out of frustration. I hated this piece of music which was complicated and, in my opinion, not worth the effort. In the silence I suddenly heard the piano playing the piece perfectly without me. My body stiffened in sheer terror as the notes echoed around the bare dusty room. Unable to stand it and, hanging around for not a second longer, I tore across the floorboards screaming and slamming the door behind me. Mum, appearing at the kitchen doorway as she heard the commotion and looking rather irritated, enquired curtly, "What on earth's going on? What all's this noise?"

"The piano's playing on its own!" I blurted out.

"Oh, for goodness sake! Stop being so stupid and making excuses and get back in there and practice."

It was the type of response I was used to. Whilst every part of my being was crying out to be rescued by her, I knew I was alone. Whilst I persisted in refusing to go anywhere near that room again to practice, mum dismissed the incident as if it had never happened, until we were visited by a well-known medium some time afterwards. In disbelief I heard mum ask her if she wouldn't mind listening to me playing the piece again. Appearing now to be interested in what had happened, mum seemed otherwise oblivious of my fear of even going in that room again. I felt saddened by the fact that she'd let me down and so, feeling under enormous pressure and anxiety, I followed the medium to the piano, led like a lamb to the slaughter.

Nothing happened. I played the piece while she sat quietly next to me on the stool with her eyes closed, trying to pick up anything that may have been hanging around us. After sensing nothing she eventually gave up and tried to reassure me, patting me on the knee and saying in a velvety voice that provided not one ounce of comfort, "It was probably just a helpful spirit trying to show you how to play the piece, dear," spoken with an air of noticeable disappointment in her voice. I was only too pleased not to have gone through the experience again even if it meant I'd disappointed them. Mum had betrayed me but it felt like I'd let her down.

And so it was that I found myself wandering up and down the aisles of trestle tables at the local jumble sale when I came across something that caught my eye. Mum and dad were on the other side of the hall when I picked up the simple pewter crucifix. Momentarily mesmerised by the cross and holding on to it tightly, I felt a sense of peace and safety wash over me. A quick search of my pockets produced enough change for it to become mine and as I tucked it away discreetly and carefully in my pocket, I scanned the hall across a sea of preoccupied people for the others.

I don't know why it caught my eye or why I thought it would save me from my fears at night, but I took that crucifix home with me in confidence. Positioning it in the centre of my windowsill, it stood on a small wooden plinth some four or five inches in height facing my bed. Every night I lay staring at it trying to block out the fear, praying the Lord's Prayer over and over until sleep would get the better of me. Often I would pick it up as I had done in the village hall, just to hold on to it for comfort.

Alone in my bedroom one weekend, I gradually became aware of the fear, a fear that was becoming increasingly familiar to me that I didn't understand. I was becoming more accustomed to these feelings and I didn't like them. Being utterly isolated by it and the thoughts going on in my mind that felt too shameful to confess, I turned and saw the crucifix out of the corner of my eye, glinting in the sun on my windowsill.   Transfixed, I walked over and lifted it down, hugging it to myself for reassurance and protection.

Resting gently in my palm it felt warm and safe. It grew warmer. Hot. The terror didn't set in immediately because my mind refused to accept what was happening.   Staring down at it in absolute disbelief, I watched as the cross began to bend itself double in my hands, burning me with its intense heat.   Feeling totally drawn into what was developing before my eyes, time seemed to stand still — but then, as if suddenly brought back to my senses, I dropped the cross to the floor while terror, shock and pain hit me all at once. I literally couldn't run fast enough down the four flights of stairs, round and round, slipping and stumbling over several steps at a time, screaming as I went until I landed in the hallway in a state of unimaginable fright — and having made quite a commotion. I couldn't turn around as I sat there in a heap for fear of what might have followed me down.

Every part of my being sensed a repulsion and disgust for what I had just witnessed through something that in my mind was supposed to protect me.   It was embarrassment that rapidly took over as it dawned on me that I would be accused of making a fuss about nothing while deep inside me my heart was crying out:

"Mummy, help me! Please make it stop!"

But nothing seemed to frighten mum and dad, and they merely laughed it off. There was nobody to turn to with this enormous fear growing inside me. Mum and dad had always told us not to tell anybody what happened at home because people wouldn't understand, but that left me isolated with no way of questioning it. I trusted them because they were my parents and I loved them, but I didn't understand why I couldn't cope with what was so obviously normal for them. If it was wrong to be afraid then I could never own up to it, but how could I live and ignore it when the fear simply swamped me every minute of every day?

♣

"Nicholas! Come back to bed!" my voice shook. To my amazement, my small six-year-old son about-turned on the stairs and started to walk back up them in silence. He was still asleep. I guided him into our own bed and waited until he had settled beside Paul before going to check on Jonathon. The air was still heavy.

Jonathon lay blissfully asleep on the top bunk in their bedroom as I crept into the bottom bunk to stay and protect our youngest child. The atmosphere in this room was particularly icy, stagnant, terribly wrong, and as I lay down I became aware of a black figure standing at the end of the bunk bed. I wanted to run back to Paul but it would mean running past the figure to do so and I didn't want to leave Jonathon alone with it. I lay there staring at it for what seemed hour upon hour, terrified and not daring to shut my eyes to sleep.

My eyes must have closed because all of a sudden I was being picked up and thrown across the room with an almighty force, crashing into the children's chest of drawers on the other side of the room. In pain and shock I opened my eyes. I was still in Nicholas's bed and the figure was still watching me. It was a dream, although there was no relief in knowing it because I had experienced it and felt the pain as if it had really happened — and the figure was still there watching me as if he had orchestrated it within my dreams. As I came to, I could hear whimpering coming from my own bedroom. It was Paul and I knew I had to help him, particularly as Nicholas was with him and it would frighten him.

The cries continued until Jonathon awoke from the noise as well and came tumbling down the ladder towards me. He saw the black figure too and screamed. Grabbing him, I made a dash past the figure and through the doorway, leaping into the bed beside the other two. Paul and Nicholas were also awake and visibly shaken by the occurrences in our own bedroom. The four of us sat huddled together with the light on for the rest of the night, Paul and I trying our best to reassure the boys and failing miserably.

As the attacks persisted night after night, the constant fear in my heart was getting the better of me. I simply couldn't go on like this anymore.

"Jesus is Lord, Jesus is Lord, Jesus is Lord, Jesus is Lord," I claimed over and over again in my mind until my teeth began to part — just a little bit, but enough for me to command through gritted teeth, "Satan, get out of here now in the name of Jesus!" The attacks always stopped with this command but I seemed to have been frightened my entire life and I'd had enough.

I curled up in a ball and let everything slip away.

♣

I was up on the third floor building a camp on the landing, a sheet fixed between the top of the banisters and two door knobs. Louisa had been playing with me in our camp but had been gone for a little before the drama unfolded. There had been no disagreement between us; she had just wandered off to do something else. I was left in the meantime playing in my own little world up there, quite content, when I became aware of a commotion coming in my direction; dad charging up the stairs. I didn't pay much attention to this until he rounded the final flight, when it dawned on me that I was somehow the purpose behind his urgency. As I sat there cross-legged on the floor, watching him lunge towards me in the most torrential rage with his voice booming at me, I couldn't make any sense of the situation. Despite the ferocious tone of his voice, I couldn't take in the words as his behaviour seemed out of place in my make believe camp, where everything had been fine a few minutes earlier. It was not as if I had hidden up there full of guilt and remorse, anticipating discipline of some kind because I didn't know what I was supposed to have done.

As I stayed put on the floor, unable and unwilling to defend myself, he grabbed hold of my arm and began hitting my thigh as hard as he could. I refused to cry, refusing to give him any satisfaction in knowing that it hurt. My body offered no resistance to the beating, it merely dangled off my arm from where he held it, resigned to its fate.

He slapped and slapped and slapped, shouting all the time, but not one word was I able to grasp. Eventually he dropped my arm and withdrew back down the stairs. Only then did I cry, silently in my room. I had no idea what I had done. There were no clues to be found in any subsequent conversations. I never questioned his anger because I didn't want to show that I cared. I had satisfaction only in knowing that I hadn't cried, although my refusal to respond had no doubt served only to stoke the fire within him.

♣

"Mummy!" Everything had faded and in a trance-like state I got up and wandered into the bathroom. I had to bring an end to the emptiness in my mind. I had to make it stop. I didn't know who I was anymore. All I could feel was a never-ending sea of inky black nothingness — a dark ocean with a determination and power of its own. But was it really nothingness?

I broke apart a razor, extracting the blade from the grip of the plastic encasing it. Where I crouched in this semi-conscious state on the bathroom floor, I began to cut. The blood began to pour long before the realisation of what I'd done could bring me back to myself. Then it dawned on me.

'I want my mummy!'

Chapter 2

The Blue Room

'**F**ERNHILL' WAS AN IMPOSING WHITE HOUSE perched on the edge of hills overlooking the valley below, with views for miles. There were seven bedrooms and two staircases, which was great fun for games of hide and seek and for smuggling out friends or boyfriends that weren't supposed to be there. Nanny and Uncle Joe had a separate annexe and our paths never crossed unless you meant them to. Louisa often spent long periods of time with them after school and during the weekend, whilst I felt imprisoned in my bedroom, alone with my thoughts.

We moved to Fernhill in the summer holidays of 1977, and come the September I was starting at secondary school. Unfortunately my class was a fairly disruptive one and being one of the few who wanted to work, it didn't actually do me any favours in the popularity stakes. At the end of the first year I had twice won the end of term merit point award, finally going on to win the overall year award across all eight classes in a year of 200 pupils. By the end of the year however I had become increasingly more depressed and unpopular. I was being teased for working hard, teased for being fat and finally, having had enough of the name-calling and lack of fun in my life, resolved to change.

It wasn't just at school where things were becoming intolerable. Life at home was becoming more bizarre. The weekly meetings continued after the move to Fernhill, taking on a new direction following the arrival of another member to the group. Ivy was a rather strange-looking emaciated woman with a puff of white hair who informed us she was from Venus. Now, instead of concentrating their efforts on communicating with spirits, they met every week in the blue room to communicate with 'superior beings from outer space'. Ivy loaned mum and dad a telescope which took up residence in the bay window of their bedroom, looking out across the valley. Every night they searched the sky for flying saucers.

"Wake up! Wake up, quickly!" came mum's voice late one night.

"Why?" I mumbled sleepily, immediately feeling a sense of impending doom.

"A flying saucer is landing tonight. Come on!"

Louisa and I were bundled out of bed and into the car in a rush, with hardly a moment to argue with her. As dad drove, mum explained that we were going to intercept a flying saucer and she was intending for us all to go off in it. As I fumbled for the door lock in terror, mum laughed announcing that I might as well not bother because aliens had telekinetic powers that could unlock car doors. I sat there, frozen to my seat, paralyzed with fear. We drove to Newlands Corner, Louisa and I in silence, where we sat on the edge of a precipice for longer than I care to remember, staring out across the pitch-black landscape. Waiting. I have no memory of getting back home again that night but clearly and mercifully we stayed earthbound.

During this period mum was taking lessons at the Spiritualist Headquarters in Belgravia to develop her psychic powers. One of the tools she invested in was a crystal ball, purchased from the Body, Mind and Spirit exhibition in London that we visited on an annual basis. Every now and again she would take herself off to her bedroom to practice, leaving instructions not to be disturbed. It was on one such occasion when Louisa and I were playing downstairs in the lounge when we heard a long protracted scream from upstairs, barely recognisable as mum. As we ran for the stairs, dad brushed us both aside, yelling brusquely, "Stay there!" as he bounded two or three steps at a time up the stairs. Glued to the spot, we stayed literally right there at the bottom of the stairs in total silence trying to listen to what was going on up there. We discovered later that as mum was using the crystal ball it had become so boiling hot that her hands had stuck to its surface. She was powerless to remove her hands as it continued to burn her flesh. I don't know how dad freed her from it but the ball was put back into its packaging and confined amongst the jumpers in mum's wardrobe.

After this event Louisa made the sudden and understandable announcement that she didn't believe in God anymore, altogether denying the existence of a spiritual world. She said that none of us were to discuss anything of a supernatural nature in her presence ever again. I knew exactly how she felt and even admired her for it, but instead I seized upon the opportunity to do something with mum and dad without her. I knew perfectly well how important it was to them so believed that if I pretended to be brave and pushed for further involvement, I could win their favour at last, but at what cost?

♣

Terrified by what I was doing, but finding myself doing it anyway, I stood staring intensely at my reflection in the wardrobe mirror. My image clouded over and there, as clearly as if he was standing in front of me, the face of a very grubby, long-haired man materialised, smirking back at me. His hair was unkempt, almost resembling dreadlocks; his skin, somewhat dark, unshaven and dirty looking.

Feeling a sense of achievement — and even anticipated acceptance — by what I had managed, I rushed downstairs to find mum. On describing him to her, she responded as if we were merely discussing the postman. "Oh yes, I've seen him around quite a bit lately. His name is Olaf," she chatted. Olaf, the strange uninvited guest, who was apparently welcome to wander around our house as and when he wanted, whoever he was! We lived in such a lovely house so how could they merely accept such an unpleasant looking person as part of the furniture? He didn't look nice to me and I wasn't at all comfortable with the thought of him wandering around just as he pleased, able to see me wherever I was, whatever I was doing, without my knowing.

Looking back now, this must seem a rather bewildering predicament; I was overwhelmed by fear associated with the psychic phenomena going on around me and knowledge that was way beyond what my young mind could cope with and yet, seeking acceptance through further involvement. My life was a dichotomy between one of privilege and apparent normality and one of unseen and unexpressed terror.

Everything in life is based upon what one initially learns as a child from one's parents and everything here was pointing towards this being normality whilst causing extreme anxiety and fear that couldn't be discussed with anyone. In the back of my mind I knew it didn't add up. Why was everyone else oblivious of this so-called 'normality'? Even then, though I knew it didn't make sense, I couldn't grasp what it was that was actually wrong. I didn't understand the depression and loneliness I was feeling and the fact that I felt desperately unloved and misunderstood. Certainly I wasn't able to make any connection between these feelings and what was going on around me.

For the most part of our lives Louisa and I went to the local school together, attended dance classes, piano lessons and belonged to the local swimming club. Whilst dad was out running the business, mum stayed at home until we both moved up to secondary school, when she then returned to her job as dad's PA. This tied in nicely with nanny coming to live with us so someone was always at home. All other aspects of our life were normal. Mum and dad never argued and seemed devoted to one another. We were never aware of any needs as we were conscious of being fortunate and so things were otherwise peaceful and stable.

But I wasn't happy.

♣

Shrieks of laughter and giggling filled the playground as the game of piggy-back chase took over the immediate vicinity. It was the latest craze.

"You're not playing because you're too fat!" a couple of chubby girls snapped in my direction, as if they had some sort of control over the game. Accepting their authority, I slunk off to sit on the steps of our classroom to watch the game, tears streaming down my face in rejection and pain. Why did the others accept what they said and how come they were allowed to play when they were bigger than me? It was just an excuse because they didn't like me, I thought — because I was different. But why was I different?

This type of thing went on all the time and I never let on to mum and dad how hard it was for me because I didn't want to disappoint them. They thought that I had lots of friends and it became such an effort to keep up the appearance in front of them. It seemed essential to make them believe that I was happy, confident and good at everything in case they rejected me and loved Louisa even more than they did already. Inside I was falling apart. How long could I keep up the pretence? I wanted their love so badly.

I was about 10 years old when I told dad that I was going to commit suicide when I grew up. "Why do you think that?" he asked. "I just have a feeling I'm going to be a drug addict and I'm going to die of an overdose," I replied, nonchalantly. I didn't say this to seek his attention, or to give him any indication of the inner sadness I felt. I felt it as if it was a curse over my life and I was stating fact; which is how dad received it.

I sat on the stairs, hugging my knees to my chest, wondering why I felt the way I did. I couldn't understand the despair and utter loneliness I felt inside. I told myself that it would get better when I reached 16, a magical age that seemed a lifetime away. I would be old enough to leave although I didn't know what I was running from.

I clambered up the shelves of the massive linen cupboards on the landing, curling up to hide like a cat amongst the sheets, blankets and pillowcases. I was lost inside my own head, awash with feelings I could make no sense of and unable to express to anybody in the world. I often came here to hide and nobody ever knew, nobody ever missed me or came looking. The house was too big to notice that I wasn't around and for that I was thankful because I didn't want them to recognise this failing in me. I didn't know how to cope and I didn't understand what I was doing but I felt safe in the cupboard. When I shut the doors it was as if I could physically shut all my fears out. This was where I would come to escape, where I curled up in the darkness struggling with the inner torture and hating myself for those feelings. Shutting down the feelings, the pain, the thoughts. Shutting everything down until the inner wrestling gradually subsided and I found solitude in nothingness.

Chapter 3

Dear Diary - 1979

SATURDAY 21 APRIL 1979. **My life changed.** Mum told me that she had been communicating with her father via the ouija board and that he said her marriage to dad had been a mistake – she was meant to be with someone else, a man who worked for dad. She told me that they had been married to each other in several previous lives and were meant to be together again.

The news was so shocking to me and I felt as if the spirit world had finally won. It felt as if everything I had been fighting against for the previous fourteen years had been for nothing.

I wanted to make mum and dad happy so they would want to stay together but I quickly found that nothing I could do would make any difference to the situation, so I gave up. In fact I blamed myself because I seemed to become completely overwhelmed by an all-consuming depression from that day and therefore incapable of much but crying. I wanted to work hard to impress them but I couldn't concentrate on anything. I wanted to make them laugh, to make them happy, but I was too depressed to make anyone happy.

With this news adding to the helplessness I already felt, I lost my appetite and interest in every aspect of my life. I went from top of my class to practically bottom. Weight fell off rapidly and I quickly developed an obsession with weight loss that became the only preoccupation to distract me from the fear and desperate unhappiness I felt inside. I managed to hide it until the end of the summer of 1979, by which point I was two stone lighter and people at school were becoming anxious. It took a teacher to report it to mum and dad before they were any the wiser, so caught up were they in their own miseries. My weight loss then became the focal point of all their frustration and anger.

It was about this time that mum and dad told me they were the reincarnations of St Peter and St Luke and that a friend of theirs was John the Baptist. They believed they communicated with St Andrew in the blue room.

♣

Saturday 21 April 1979: *'In the afternoon I was sitting talking to mum. I know I said a couple of days ago that I felt my life was about to change, well it happened today. Anyway, mum told me that Ken keeps telling her she must leave dad and go to this other bloke who she was married to in another life, on the ouija board. She loves him and he loves her and the love has been brought forward from hundreds of years ago to now. She's been going mad with worry and has had to have drugs and injections to calm her down. Dad is heartbroken of course and everything is a nightmare. I can't stop crying - it really is terrible.'*

Saturday 16 June 1979:   *It's been such a horrible day. Horrible, horrible day. Cry, cry, cry! That's all I live to do — cry! It's all I'm fit for. To start with, mum was on the verge of walking out on us. It's Fraser — she was being so stupid. She won't even try to forget him at all and I was shouting at her and she was crying. Dad shouted at her then I was crying. They went out and I stayed at home on my own. How come if they are the disciples they have got themselves into such a mess and are so unhappy?*

I think I'm in love with PB but he doesn't want me. Do you understand that? He doesn't want me. He was rotten to me on the phone when he rang. He broke my heart with what he said. It wasn't much but to me it was everything. He doesn't care about me. It's lies, lies, LIES. And I'm crying again now. Don't you understand that I want to love you? I don't care if it kills me because I want to make you happy. Crying again now - nobody wants me or cares about me. I've had a horrible day and nobody is going to make it better, nobody is going to make my life worth living except PB. And that's not going to happen until he cares for me, takes me in his arms, loves me, until he cares for me. When will he ever understand me; my sensitive heart that's continually being broken by his hard uncaring heart?

I wish I were made of metal and lived in another world where emotions don't exist and dreams of love aren't even heard of. God, why did you invent us like this? Why? Why? Why? It's hell. Someone help me, please help me. I'm going to start something serious soon. I don't know what — pills, drink, something. I'm already anorexic and I've lost half a stone in the last couple of days through love, pain, anger and worrying so much that it's going to kill me, I know.   I want to die and I'm going to die.   No-one cares. Nobody loves me and I love everyone far too easy.

He says he loves me but why doesn't he show it, why doesn't he want to give me his love?   He doesn't love me. I don't understand and it just hurts like a spear being pushed through my heart - so slow.   I feel so awful now, I really do. I tried to kill myself.   I feel like a seven-year-old, I feel so bloody bad.   I want L (friend) now.   I want to go round her house now.   I need her.   L, you're the only one who can help me now.'

Tuesday 19 June 1979:   *'Horrid day as always, all my days are horrid at this school.   Mr R was getting at me the whole time in History.   He gave me lines to do.   He kept calling me out all the time in front of the class to tell me off about something else.   After lesson he gave me a long lecture on things, my work, teachers worried about me.   It's not my fault.   It's all mum's with her ***ing affair.   And on top of the lines paper I wrote about it to tell him because he said if I have a problem then I must tell him.   I was crying as he said it and as I went to French I was crying.   I gave him the lines, grabbed my coat and RAN.'*

Friday 6 July 1979:   *'Got told off in French as usual and I had to sit on my own at the front.   I hate that lesson, it's so pathetic.   I used to like it and do well, now I don't care a damn and haven't done any homework for her, hardly ever. No lunch as usual.   I must lose more and more weight.   They all say I'm too skinny but they don't know – nobody does. I've got to lose OVER another half a stone.'*

Tuesday 10 July 1979:   *'I went to school, planning all the time where I was going to go.   By the middle of the morning I couldn't stand anymore and told Jill I was leaving at lunch-time.   She said she'd come, so at lunch-time we just walked out.   We went to my house and climbed through the cellar window and up into the kitchen.   We got clothes and got a train to Egham.   We camped out in a graveyard and at about 9pm I telephoned L.   She told me mum and dad had got the police out and they were crying and everything, so I told her where we were.   She rang them and told them and at about 10pm mum turned up with the dog looking for us.'*

Sunday 29 July 1979:   *'Today mum, dad and me went to Bobby's christening – he is mum's best friend Annette's baby – well, he is a space child given to her when they took her and gave her a special operation aboard one of their ships.   That is, the space people took her.   Only mum, dad, Annette and I know this.   Annette told us everything about when they had taken her spiritually through astral travel and given her this child when she didn't know what they were doing or why.'*

Friday 3 August 1979:   *'Dad took me and Louisa to an Italian restaurant which I couldn't possibly get out of.   Mum was in London for the night.   Seeing as I wouldn't be eating for days I made a real pig of myself.   I had a pizza and half of Louisa's cannelloni, a coke and an orange sorbet.   And I still wasn't full – when I start to eat I get hungrier and hungrier.   When I got home I saw food and couldn't stop myself - I had to eat more.   I had some raspberry and chocolate yoghurt and two thirds of a tin of tuna.   I was so hungry, I just couldn't stop at all.   I was so cross with myself afterwards.   Late that night a very old friend of dad's called* *by unexpectedly. He was one of the first who came to their group but has not come for a very long time now. I don't know what he came for, perhaps to see if he would be allowed back in. But they have stopped the group because they began to get a bad atmosphere with mum gallivanting around. Anyway lots of the old ones want to join again – I don't know what they'll do.'*

Sunday 12 August 1979: *'We got up early today to go to Bournemouth to visit Jan (John the Baptist) – I've told you of her. It was St Peter, St Luke, St Thomas's niece, Ruth and John the Baptist and another person from that time that I don't know the name. We went to the sea first at Sandbanks before going to their house. Mum had brought a picnic and so I had to have a quarter of a sandwich and a shrivelled up sausage to keep them quiet. No drink. I sat and read all the time — a book about a girl called Mary in the 19th century who was possessed. I've got a terrible hunch that I'm that girl reincarnated. I don't know for sure but it feels as if I'm reading about myself. It also makes me cry because it's so sad.*

Later we went to Jan's and everyone had tea - I had nothing - dad kept making fun of me because I wasn't hungry. I didn't speak to any of them today; I just locked myself in a shell and lived in my own private world because I don't like them. I'll never love them, never. I think there was a great mistake somewhere.

In the evening Jan gave me a choc-ice. I ate it and then went straight upstairs and sicked it up. I'm getting good with my food now.'

Tuesday 14 August 1979: '*I stayed in bed until after lunch reading the book mum gave me about Mary Roff, who was possessed and died suddenly at the age of 19 – she then took over the body of another girl who was having a similar problem 12 years later to protect her. I am the reincarnation of Mary Roff. You must read the book and find out it is true. I tell you, I know. I cried all morning as I read that book as I remembered scenes, and then called out to my find my mum from my past life. I had to find her somehow.*

I rang dad at work and through fits of tears I eventually managed to tell him. At first he said, "You've got a rich imagination my girl!" but when I screamed at him, he knew I was being serious. He came home immediately. While I was waiting for him I nearly took an overdose. I had to get to my mum and that was the only way.

When dad got home I was still in fits of tears and I told him that we must do the Christos so I can get back there (and then when I get there, I will stay there and not come back at all, but I won't tell them that or they won't let me go back at all). Dad said we'll do it when mum agrees at the right time. He took me to gran's for the afternoon. Gran and dad had lunch and pudding and I had none, much to gran's worries and constant persuasion. I had some chocolate late afternoon but went upstairs and sicked it up. At tea-time at home, mum made a very big meal but I sicked that up too. It's the only way to keep them off my back and hide this.'

Tuesday 28 August 1979: '*Today I was being horrible to everybody as usual. I'm so moody and I feel so weak and ill.*'

Thursday 6 September 1979: '*It's been an absolutely terrible day. Never in all my thoughts or dreams would I* *have ever thought this could happen. As usual I went and left all my friends at dinner and went to read. When they came out they told me that they were all terribly worried about me – my eating – and during lunch, while discussing it, Jill was crying and so she had gone to tell Mrs R EVERYTHING. I felt so sick as I heard this and after talking, they realised she shouldn't have gone that far so we went to find her but couldn't. As we were standing waiting for her to return and give the verdict, Mrs R approached and asked me what I'd eaten today and yesterday for lunch. I told her the truth so she said immediately she was going to tell mum as there was no flesh on me. I burst into tears for the rest of break and everyone was trying to reassure me it was for the best as they really cared about me. Anyway after Smike rehearsals tonight, without any warning, mum drove me straight to the doctors. At first I was scared and cross, especially as I've decided to stop now and the only reason I have had no lunch was so I could get more money to buy mum and dad a beautiful Christmas present. And I've had salad and chicken for tea at home too yesterday. I told mum this and she told me not to tell the doctor – she didn't want to look a fool, an over-worrying mother, so I said nothing. But when I tried to explain how about a year ago I was really fat and that I'd kept my stomach in all the time so people thought I was slim, which I certainly wasn't, he didn't listen to a single word. Instead he's referred me to a psychiatrist. I was crying when I came out and I swore like hell about him to mum and we both cried bitterly all the way home. She knows he was wrong to talk like that but also that I am ill, which I'm not. I was so fat and only now am I getting a decent figure. Only my legs and arms were slim before and so they've got thin and that's what's done it. If I had the choice I'd do it a bit more but I can't possibly and they're going to make me so fat. I'll be a laughing stock! HELP ME PLEASE. Nobody understands. For the first time I told my secret to mum that I wasn't really slim at all and was just holding my tummy in but she won't accept it. She still says I'm very ill and need help. Yes, I need help, to STOP me getting this treatment! I'm so scared in case they make me fat again. I ate a biscuit tonight with a cup of tea and I had cold chicken with salad for tea just to prove to them I'm not ill — Oh help me, PLEASE.'*

Saturday 22 September 1979:   *'This morning mum kept coming in and telling me to get up so she could weigh me. I shouted at her and after half an hour she called dad, who came in screaming at me so loud I was scared. In the end they tipped the mattress up, grabbed me and dragged me to the bathroom and shoved me on the scales. I was 6 stones. They carried on screaming and shouting at me and I got dressed quickly and got all my homework together to take it to do at the library. I wouldn't speak to either of them so it started another row. I just cycled off at about 9am. I worked until about 12.15 and then I met Amanda. I had to be back home at 1pm or they'd kill me. I was so scared that she agreed to come back to my house for lunch so as to keep them away from me. I ate my lunch without potatoes and didn't eat afters like them. Mum and dad went out and I went to Amanda's house later and left a note saying I was having tea there, which I wasn't.'*

Sunday 23 September 1979:   *'This morning I got up very early. I couldn't sleep last night. I went to bed at 9.30 p.m. as I was tired but I woke at 11 p.m., 3a.m., 4 a.m., 5 a.m. and*

*then at 6 a.m, I gave up and read a book. I got up at 7 a.m. to
go to Holy Communion. I am going to get confirmed.'*

♣

"Our Father who art in heaven, hallowed be thy name…"
I'm so frightened, I can't shut my eyes. I can't turn the light
off because then I won't be able to see. But I can't see *them*
with the light on either, even though I know they're here.
I'm so tired, but I can't sleep because if I lose control then
they might get me. I can't put my legs out straight because
then my feet will be too near the end of the bed and I can't
see what's at the end of the bed. They might pull me out by
my feet. I have to keep as small as I can be.

"Thy kingdom come, thy will be done, on earth as it is in
heaven…" I'm so frightened. Jesus please help me.

"Give us this day our daily bread…" Please help me to
starve and lose more weight.

"And forgive us our sins as we forgive those who sin
against us. Lead us not into temptation and deliver us from
evil…" Please don't let them get me Lord. Please make
them go away.

"For thine is the kingdom, the power and the glory,
forever and ever, Amen. Our Father who art in heaven,
hallowed by thy name…"   Dear Lord God, I'm so
frightened. Please help me. Please help me….'

Every night the same routine: absolute terror, curled up
in a ball, repeating the Lord's Prayer over and over until
sleep eventually got the better of me.

Chapter 4

Bathed in Love

I T WAS A DARK and dreary weekend as I lay in the bath feeling miserable and very lonely. The faint watery light from the sun just managed to glint off the bubbles of distorted glass. Staring at it, I found myself praying and asking Jesus to come into my life. I had been attending confirmation classes and although this may seem like an odd thing to have done in the circumstances, dad had always spoken about Jesus to me. He had his own views as to who Jesus was but certainly recognised Him as somebody we should try to model ourselves upon. Whenever I had been naughty he would say to me, "What would Jesus do?" much to my annoyance. Unfortunately it became an expression I came to hate. It was Jesus however that I turned to for help with my fear during these early years.

As I gazed at the faint sunlight glistening on the bathroom window, a ball of light seemed to come through the glass. Increasing in brightness and size as I stared at it in wonder, the light began to descend until I found myself completely engulfed in luminous golden rays. As if everything was happening in slow motion, two hands materialised in glowing brilliance. Momentarily suspended within the light, the hands then came to rest on each of my own hands before disappearing through my skin. Feeling as if arms were reaching down inside my own, as if mine were merely the sleeves, and fingers filled my own as if I were the gloves, I lay in supreme awe.

I felt completely at peace and at no moment did I feel the least afraid, despite all previous experiences. I knew deep within me that I was experiencing God's love in a particularly special way and I knew that the hands belonged to Jesus. My whole body was washed through with His love and peace, filling every part of me. I lay there bathing in His light and warmth, enjoying every second of it. It was the most beautiful vision and experience I have ever had and it is impossible to really put into words the sheer beauty and magnitude of what had taken place. I held on to this experience secretly within my heart, unwilling to share it for fear of it being devalued.

My love for Jesus became simply overwhelming, as in that moment I had been made aware of His love for me too. It outweighed any emotional feelings of love that I had ever known. I knew it would probably seem like any other psychic experience to mum and dad, but I knew that this had been different. I held it close to me with a safe knowledge that I had experienced Jesus in a very special way that was personal for me alone. I needed to know He was there and I wasn't alone and He knew.

My baptism and confirmation were profoundly moving as again, I experienced moments of His golden warmth and closeness to me within the oppressive bleakness of spiritualism, and divorce.

Despite this, there were aspects of Christianity that failed to make any sense to me. I had been brought up to believe that we had another dimension to our faith that Christians denied existence of, the parallel existence of a spirit world filled with our loved friends and relatives watching over us and the reality of psychic phenomena. As I had first hand experience, I found myself struggling to accept Christianity as a single faith. Many years passed before I came to understand the difference between what Christians understand as demonic warfare and that which Spiritualists embrace - and the danger of exposing yourself to such forces. I was steeped in lies muddying the clear water of God's truth and a long way off from discovering it.

Chapter 5

An Escape Route

LIFE WAS COMPLICATED at home and I was far from well. Everybody was extremely stressed and unfortunately Dad seemed to focus all his frustrations on my eating. Mum was confusing me by coming to me for personal advice and reassurance for her actions; should she stay with Dad or leave to go with Fraser? Which one did I like best, Dad or Fraser? And would I go with her if she went with Fraser?

Deciding to use the situation to my own advantage, I told mum that I would go with her and Fraser if she promised to stop all my treatment for the anorexia. To my surprise this was an acceptable deal. What I wasn't aware of was that the psychiatrist had met with mum and dad alone and whilst the blue room remained shrouded in secrecy, they had discussed the impending divorce. Dr Field had had stern words to say about the way they were handling the situation and mum was not happy about having the blame pointed directly at her, so she was very compliant with my request to end treatment. Dr Field had been given the impression that I had stopped eating long before I became aware of the affair and that there had been no cause to suspect anything to be unduly wrong until that point, which wasn't true.

Not long afterwards mum, Fraser and I moved into rented accommodation in Hartley Wintney until we were able to move into a small house mum was buying in Bagshot. The rented cottage, once nothing more than a stable, wasn't especially welcoming or homely, particularly as most of our things went into storage for the time being. Following my persuasions, Louisa, who was thirteen by then, went to live with dad — I suggested this was only fair so he wasn't left on his own.

Dad had been seeing one of the secretaries at work while mum had been seeing Fraser and, not long after the divorce came through, Nanette and her own two children moved in with dad and Louisa. I think mum found this particularly hard, as did Louisa of course, and to compensate for this she took her out on Saturdays and bought her things. With no compassion or understanding of Louisa's own predicament, I struggled instead to deal with my jealousy. I merely wanted Louisa out of the way in order to have my mum to myself and I think I felt glad at her discomfort; glad I was having no more treatment, glad I was left to my own devices. Life on the whole continued to be a bewildering mix of emotions and bizarre circumstances.

One particular weekend after one of their shopping trips mum brought Louisa back to the cottage for the first time. Feeling immediately resentful and intensely jealous, all the suspicious thoughts I harboured of being loved less flooded my mind. Seizing mum's tranquillizers from her bedside drawer, I retreated to my room determined to make it all go away. I knew in that moment how to make it stop. I had a tiny room barely bigger than the single bed I lay on. Apart from the bed and my hi-fi, the room was otherwise empty with white-washed walls and blue vinyl on the floor. I turned on the hi-fi and started swallowing mum's pills. As I lay on the bed I drifted back to my old room at Fernhill. In my mind I stood looking at my desk scattered with books, pictures of ponies pinned to the board behind. I turned to see the pale yellow flowers on the walls, the vanity unit in the corner, the pale cream carpet on the floor; carpet that I'd been proud to tell my friends that Prince Charles had walked on at one of dad's exhibitions! All the things that were special to me had gone. This room smelt damp and as I lay on the bed crying quietly, longing for it all to end, I slipped into a deep sleep.

Forceful shaking eventually brought me back to my senses. "Beverley, wake up now, do you hear me? This isn't funny so stop messing around and get up!" It was dark outside and I was unsure how long I had been asleep for. They were angry with me and made me sit at the table with them whilst they talked in order to keep me awake. Slipping in and out of their conversations, deeply resentful and past caring, I longed to be left alone. The thought that I actually wanted to die had taken root. They had no idea of the quantity of pills I had actually taken and strangely, the question was never asked so it was never taken as a suicide attempt.

The following day mum agreed to let me stay home from school because I felt ill, telling me to stay in bed and rest while she went to work. I spent the day in a complete daze with uncontrollable crying. The week continued on in much the same way so mum sent me to stay with a friend of hers while she was at work.

As we stood at the tills in a shop, mum's friend preoccupied with paying, waves of darkness suddenly overwhelmed me and I fainted. That evening mum finally took me to the doctor. He told her I should have been seen on Sunday to have my stomach washed out and how dangerous it had been for someone of my age — I was lucky to be alive. He talked over me, never to me, not asking me why or how I felt, leaving me feeling that I'd done something naughty and distasteful. *My* feelings didn't matter. They never had.

This event seemed to have a surprising effect on how people related to me. Mum had obviously told some of her friends, including Annette, who lived next door. Some of her friends seemed to become very cautious and wary of me and Annette even said I was not to visit them. I couldn't understand why she felt like this when I had stayed with them on several occasions to baby-sit for her children. I didn't realise then that I could be used as a means of gaining attention and sympathy because the idea that my feelings were something to be ashamed of and should remain concealed, had become entrenched within me. The fact that I had gone some way towards revealing them and the subsequent reaction they brought, served only to reinforce this belief.

One night, while mum and Fraser were out and I was left on my own in that horrible cottage, I decided to walk round to Annette's for some company, despite having been told not to. I knew that their niece was staying with them and she was only slightly older than me. Outside was pitch black and between the two cottages was a long, dark and muddy lane to negotiate. I was scared of the dark but the thought of reaching them, as opposed to spending the evening on my own in that cottage, made the journey seem worthwhile. With my heart pounding, and feeling a huge sense of relief as I reached for the doorbell, I wasn't prepared for what happened next.

As the door opened, I was greeted by the end of a rifle pointing straight at me. Facing me was Rick, Annette's husband, and as I looked at him in disbelief he shouted: "Get off my land before I shoot you!" Annette was standing in the background of the kitchen and I expected her to tell Rick to stop it, to laugh or something, but she said nothing. I turned and fled back into the darkness of the lane without looking back, frightened, ashamed and very confused.

I knew their niece had recently been diagnosed with cancer and I assumed they thought I must be really selfish to have taken an overdose. Because I knew I wasn't supposed to go round there in the first place, I decided to avoid telling mum - although I realised it would only be a matter of time before she found out for herself. Not long afterwards, mum reported that dad had apparently said that I wasn't to go near his house either. I assumed that he had disowned me on account of my behaviour too.

All I could imagine was that I had to be such a bad person if he didn't love me anymore. I was hurting inside so much that I didn't know what to do with all the pain — except to focus all my attention on starving and losing weight.

By the time we moved to our new home I was fifteen and in my final year at school. G.C.E.'s were looming but life was far too confusing and depressing to care about such things as G.C.E.'s. It seemed that nobody cared about me or took an interest in whether I studied or not despite the fact that I had previously been more than capable. Concentration now an impossible task, I spent lessons sitting in a dream world, cutting myself off from pretty much everything. Anorexia was unheard of in school then and there were several rumours going around suggesting that I was a drug addict, even though none of us had ever seen a drug addict either. I couldn't be bothered to enlighten them. I was given the nickname 'Snapper' by the boys in my class and often overheard them laughing, or yelling at me to watch out in case the wind blew because I might snap in half. I tried to ignore it all.

Although I'd always been pretty rubbish at sport, I joined the school hockey and athletics clubs so that I could burn up as many calories as possible at lunchtime. Even on the days when there were no clubs I still ran around the field during my lunch hour pretending to be serious about improving upon my performance. I must admit that I was amazed that Mrs Robins, who was my form teacher as well as one of the P.E. teachers, allowed me to do it. P.E. which was in the sports hall using the apparatus was an unpleasant experience though. My body would be racked with pain when we had to lie on the floor mats for warm up exercises. My spine was so prominent that, despite the mats, the floor caused me considerable discomfort. Not wanting to draw any more attention to myself, I used to persevere and tried so hard to keep the pain from showing on my face.

In the midst of all this suffering and unhappiness I found an oasis in the form of music. I played the clarinet with my friend Amanda in the school band but my real passion lay with singing and one day I got the opportunity to front the school band. Following the success of this, my music teacher put together an adult band which included friends of his and he asked me to sing with them. It was a proper group, consisting of a guitarist, drummer, bassist and my teacher on keyboards. This was something I thought was worth living for at last! Initially the group was formed in order to take part in a national schools' competition but we also began rehearsing for the finale at the end of year school concert.

I didn't think it the least bit odd when one of my teacher's friends, Neil, the guitarist in the band, asked me if I would like to meet him in London after school. Rather, I was excited at the prospect despite the fact that he was in his twenties and I was still fifteen. He even had a car and it wasn't long before I became infatuated. Neil still lived with his parents and I began spending a lot of time there with him listening to music and writing our own songs. The other members of the group joined us at weekends as we prepared for the concert. Mum liked Neil, probably liking the fact that he took me off her back for most of the weekend as much as anything.

Neil had other things on his mind though and it wasn't long before I found myself out of depth. When the relationship became a sexual one I thought that I was mature and in control of the situation. Despite the fact that mum was fully aware that the relationship had moved on, she would phone Neil and ask him to come and get me when I was particularly depressed. He was abusing me and feelings of disgust and self-hatred intensified. I scratched at my skin with needles, dyed my hair and wore a lot of heavy make-up to school. Sometimes a teacher told me to wash my face but I couldn't go out without it. It became yet another mask to hide behind. I couldn't leave Neil because then I wouldn't be able to sing in the band and I needed to hang on to that. I felt completely trapped, which was a very familiar feeling for me.

By allowing the situation to continue, I began to see it as just another way of abusing myself. One day I rang up one of the other band members and asked him out. I didn't like Gary at all but I knew that he fancied me even though he had his own girlfriend. That first evening we had sex and for the first time I had used another person to hurt myself and it left me feeling even more disgusting - but this at least rang true with what everyone already seemed to think about me. Because I had orchestrated the evening there was an element of satisfaction, of feeling in control. I didn't consider Gary's feelings because I saw it as giving him something he wanted and I really don't know what he thought. He was taking cannabis and so it wasn't long before he introduced me to smoking it. Neil didn't know that I'd been seeing Gary but the friction between us by then was pretty awful. We were no longer 'going out' as such, although the relationship hadn't come to an end because I didn't want to sabotage my chances of singing in the band and so sleeping with Gary as well became a safety net in case it all went wrong. The first afternoon that Gary brought cannabis to the group practice we got completely stoned and Neil took advantage of the situation by raping me in front of Gary and I was too drugged to stop it. This signalled a turning point but not in any positive sense: I was pure worthlessness and deserved it.

There was also a turning point at home when, out of the blue, Fraser walked out on mum. He simply vanished into thin air leaving mum to collapse into a state of depression herself, spending all the time she wasn't at work in her bed crying. To make matters worse Dad and Nanette got married around about the same time.

So the G.C.E.'s came and went and I didn't bother doing any revision. Worse still, I didn't even bother turning up for one of them. I had no plans whatsoever for the future. I left school at sixteen and watched on from a distance as my friends moved on with their lives; Amanda went off to college to do a pre-nursing course, Marie and Sarah both got secretarial jobs in Woking, whilst others went on to college. Mum pestered me to look for work but I didn't want to know.

I had done so badly at school in the end and I looked such a complete mess that I really didn't stand a chance of getting a job. With school over and the only routine I had gone, I stayed in bed all day instead, consumed with depression and the sense of hopelessness growing ever deeper.

I thought of ways of escaping my life and one of the ideas I came up with was modelling. I wanted to enrol at a modelling college in London but both mum and dad refused to pay for it. Neil had been pushing me for some time to go away for a week with him to his parent's holiday home in Cornwall and mum offered the dreadful idea that I could go with him if he agreed to pay the college fees. By then I hated Neil so much, but I desperately wanted to escape and this presented the only means of achieving it. So reluctantly I agreed to go along with it. Little did I anticipate what lay in store as I spent a week at his mercy tied up and left in a room in complete darkness, with him returning only to abuse me. When I ate I wasn't allowed to leave the room to be sick and so was forced to throw up in carrier bags. As I stood in the shower, frightened and abandoned, he insisted that I urinate there and then in front of him and because he had taken total control away from me, I wet myself.

I blamed mum and dad for not loving me and for allowing it to happen. I had been exploited but believed that I deserved it by agreeing to go away with him for money. I had humiliated myself and felt it was my own fault. I did not go on to become a model. There had been no escape route after all.

Chapter 6

Fold Me Up

AFTER A COUPLE OF MONTHS of cajoling I took a boring clerical position in a drawing office on a temporary basis. Danny was one of several contract draughtsmen. He stood out because of his long hair and extremely casual dress sense. Most of the men were fairly casual anyway but Danny wore brightly coloured trousers that were simply cut off at the bottom and fraying. Every lunch-time we went to the local pub with a crowd from the office and the men delighted in buying me no end of drinks. Being unaccustomed to alcohol and having downed 5 or 6 vodkas in the hour, I would return to the office worse for wear, much to the disgust of the older women in my department. I hated the job so I didn't care, but the lunch breaks became good fun and almost worth going to work for.

When I discovered that Danny played guitar in a band, I knew that I had found my chance to escape from Neil at last. Before long I had talked a little about what was going on at home and Danny was genuinely concerned and promised to ring me when he got back home from a gig. That evening mum had been in an hysterical state for most of the time and by the time Danny rang around midnight, I was sitting downstairs by the telephone waiting and crying. "Pack your things," he whispered down the telephone, "I'm coming to get you!"

As I gathered a few things together, I could hear my mother's continuous sobbing coming from her bedroom. In one sense it should have been awful that her daughter was leaving her as well but I think instead it probably came as a relief. I left it until I knew Danny would be nearly there before going in to tell her that I was leaving. It met with no reaction; she didn't ask any questions, made no attempt to stop me or to ask me where I was going. I couldn't stand it any longer even if it meant I was walking out on her as well and when Danny turned up finally at 1 o'clock in the morning in a taxi, I turned my back on everything and walked away. I desperately wanted to escape and start a new life.

Danny was eight years older than me and divorced, whilst I had turned seventeen two weeks before I left home to be with him. We needed to find somewhere suitable to live and we began trawling around estate agents until we found an old, very poorly furnished cottage on the outskirts of a small village miles from anywhere, surrounded by fields of cows. Initially it seemed idyllic but without the use of a car it was a totally unrealistic choice, albeit a cheap one. Whilst I felt some relief and happiness at getting away from it all, and even managed to gain some weight for a while, clearly I was still very unwell. Danny proposed to me and I couldn't have been happier with the prospect of marrying him and the security in knowing I had escaped forever.

Danny had quite a social life, having lived in the same area all his life, and every night of the week consisted of pub-crawls and drink. Everyone seemed so happy which conflicted with everything I'd gone through and I really struggled to feel part of his social group. I was enthusiastic to start with about eventually fitting in, but soon lost heart as I became acutely aware of how different my life was to theirs. The girls still lived at home, despite being quite a bit older than me and I found myself feeling very envious of the apparent stability of their lives. One of them worked with her father from home for his design company; she was such a character, the life and soul of every evening. In fact she seemed so happy that it hurt.

Contact with Dad was virtually non-existent and I hardly ever saw mum or Louisa either. I began to write long letters to my old friends, to Marie and Sarah who were enjoying their jobs in Woking and to Amanda who told me all about life at college. I told them how much I loved Danny and about our music, but in reality their lives seemed full whilst mine was so empty and the contrast was a painful reminder of how messed up my life was. Their letters became a lifeline even though I couldn't bear to see them and avoided meeting up with them.

I was so in love with Danny but he was never at home and it began to feel like I wasn't alive when he wasn't there. My anxieties now manifested as agoraphobia. Danny, on the other hand, continued to go out so I spent more and more time alone and the situation grew worse. The agoraphobia developed into paranoia as I spent more and more hours alone in the house, feeling abandoned and desperately lonely. As the days, weeks and months passed, I became afraid of ever going out again. I never opened the front door, living in terrible fear of anyone ever coming to the house. I stayed in bed all day only getting washed and dressed before Danny came home in the evening. But he was only ever in the house briefly before he went back out for a drink, regardless of the fact that I was unable to accompany him anymore.

The cottage was filthy, the furniture sparse. We had no vacuum cleaner, no heating and no fridge. I became convinced that the house was haunted and could not bear to go up to the third floor alone. If I heard anything or thought anyone might be coming to the house, I hid underneath the bed. My thoughts were playing havoc with me and I became convinced that Danny was going to kill me for some unknown reason, despite the fact that he had never been violent. I hid all the kitchen knives and insisted that he walked up the stairs in front of me so I could see him. I couldn't even turn my back on him in bed in fear of him stabbing me. I tried to conceal the extent of the irrationality in case it triggered an attack from him, but he just seemed amused by my idiosyncrasies, as he saw them. Nobody knew the extent of what was actually going on in my mind as I battled with misery and tortured thoughts by escaping for hours on end into periods of nothingness, as I had learnt to do as a child in the airing cupboard.

At weekends we worked in the studio we had created on the top floor. We continued to write our own songs and record them and I continuously begged Danny to give up his job, to stay at home with me and to have a go at going professional. Eventually he agreed! Not only were we going to be together constantly, we were also going to be spending all of our time on the one thing that mattered to both of us, as we actually shared our passion for music. The only problem was that if Danny gave up his job we wouldn't be able to pay the rent and so, with some trepidation, we went back to Mum and asked if she would let us both move in for a while so that we could get it off the ground.

Returning home with Danny to work on our music full time made the prospect of a future in the music industry actually seem possible. My paranoia and agoraphobia naturally subsided although my eating disorder persisted; weight gained briefly at the beginning of our relationship had soon fallen back off once I'd been left alone in the cottage. Naïvely we thought it would be no time at all before we had ourselves a major record deal and our lives would turn around for the better.

Unfortunately our lives as professional musicians weren't all that they were cracked up to be. Danny and I moved into the box room at mum's with all our recording gear, a cat and a litter tray. There was barely enough room to move, not alone write music and rehearse in there. Neither of us were particularly pro-active at getting work, although we did perform the occasional gig, preferring to concentrate our efforts instead on securing a record deal. This of course did not provide any money in the short-term.

It was the age of the New Romantics and accordingly we looked and dressed in such a way that alone got us into the papers. Of course I was thin, my hair was bleached white and back-combed into a wild, punk style whilst I wore very short skirts and lace that I'd put together myself. The local paper described me as a punk ballerina. Danny also dyed his hair blond and wore frilly shirts.

After more than a year of disappointments and rejections, the hours spent in recording studios paid off and the contract we had dreamt of finally arrived. We were signed to an indie label belonging to the family of a major recording artist and began work on our first single. 'Fold Me Up' was written when we had been living in the cottage and summed up the angst and madness I'd experienced at the time. It described how I felt like an item of clothing put away in a drawer when Danny wasn't with me, taken out briefly and worn upon his return before being put away again. The melody was simple but the lyrics would have made no sense to anybody other than me.

A lot of the backing tracks for 'Fold Me Up' were laid down in a studio in North London, whilst the vocals were recorded at a brand new studio in Fulham. As we entered what resembled a Greek temple on the inside, excitement and anticipation were hard to contain but were quickly shattered before the end of the night. It rapidly became apparent that we had a problem with our engineer who, whilst sitting at the mixing desk, drank his way through an entire bottle of neat Vodka throughout the course of the night. We returned home frustrated and tired, adamant that we would never work with him again but what we hadn't picked up on was the fact that he and the producer who'd signed us were lovers. We wanted a new engineer but when we returned to discuss the situation we found them in bed together and complaining about his drunken behaviour in the studio didn't go down well. Disenchanted with each other, we parted company, failing to complete the recording of 'Fold Me Up'.

The contract we had signed unfortunately stated that we were forbidden from recording 'Fold Me Up' for a two-year period for any other company, which came as a huge blow when we realised the implications. The ensuing despondency made it virtually impossible to write anything else and Danny made the decision to return to work as we were totally broke.

A friend of ours who regularly helped out as a roadie for our gigs persuaded us to house share with him and his partner. They had another lodger and it seemed like a good idea and we needed some fun. But once behind closed doors these friends really took us by surprise. There was no heating in the house and the carpet was so damp that it squelched under your feet as you trod on it. One weekend, in order to deal with the freezing temperatures in the house, our housemates resorted to taking the lounge door off, sawing it up on the carpet and throwing it onto a fire! A thick, foul smoke filled the house as Danny and I shut ourselves away in our room in disbelief.

With Danny and the others out at work during the day, I was left at home alone again. I was painfully thin and as the cold got to me it became uncomfortable to walk. At the same time I started to binge on vast quantities of food during the day, only to make myself sick immediately afterwards before anyone returned home. My life felt out of control again and our living conditions were making it worse. Rather than look for somewhere else to rent, we decided to buy a studio flat and whilst this meant Danny would have to continue working full time, it gave us the security of a clean and comfortable home of our own at last.

In the summer of 1984, when I was 19 years old, we were married. It was a small wedding, attended only by our immediate family and a handful of friends, followed by a weekend away in Cornwall. Before the wedding had even taken place, doubts had begun to set in but the merry-go-round that I was on was getting faster and faster, with no apparent hope of getting off. My identity had become so interwoven with such a wild cacophony of emotions and irrational beliefs that there was no room for love anymore.

Danny was working inordinately long hours, travelling by train to London each day via a country service that was notoriously slow. Sometimes I drove him to the station in the morning just to ease the monotonous routine I was stuck in. My days were long and consisted entirely of trying to stop the obsessive-compulsive thoughts in my head, which was impossible. I stayed in bed for as long as I could, followed by spending the remaining hours curled up in a chair without moving from it because if I did, it would mean moving in the direction of the kitchen. There was only one small living area in the studio flat with a kitchen and bathroom leading off it. We didn't own a television and the obsessive thoughts prevented me from reading, so there was no distraction. Getting up from the chair was to lose control because if I got up, it would lead to eating; this would lead to feelings of guilt, which coupled with being so ravenously hungry, lead to eating everything we had in an uncontrollable frenzy. I would literally eat until I was unable to stand any longer from the pain and weight in my stomach, forcing me to crawl to the bathroom to make myself sick.

When this happened it felt like I was possessed by something beyond myself, a wild force that I was unable to control. It was as if I stepped outside of myself to look on in disgust and horror at the person who was stuffing herself with everything she could lay her hands on. This person wasn't me and I hated her for her lack of control and filthy habits, for needing food and for putting it into a body that I wanted to deny and destroy. Another part of me was glad that the binge was so uncontrollable so that my encounter with food was not a pleasant one. But, it served a purpose as this behaviour built a wall between me and my memories. My mind was focused on something other than what had happened in the past and whilst I still had to sleep with the light on, I wasn't in touch with the reason why in quite the same way.

A battle was going on, although I wasn't sure which side I was on; had I succumbed to being taken over by an outside force or was I simply trying to punish myself for being so hungry?

I hated the routine and futility of my life. The whole bingeing process could take well over an hour which resulted in feelings of total self-disgust and a sense of utter failure, as well as physical exhaustion. I would collapse onto my bed in floods of tears at the loss of control, desperate at that point for someone to help me. When I wasn't bingeing, on the other hand, I didn't want any help because the thoughts and fears associated with gaining weight outweighed any potential benefits I could see.

It was the intensity of the bingeing that eventually took me to the doctors. I was terrified of asking for help and admitting to my behaviour, not least because of the sense of failure I felt at having not managed to starve to death after the length of time I'd been ill.

Asking for help marked the beginning of a new era and the commencement of what was to be a long drawn out period of psychiatric treatment. I was referred to Dr Wood, a tall slightly balding Consultant Psychiatrist from New Zealand, who lacked the bedside manner of my new GP, Dr Marks, but upon whom nevertheless, I was to become hopelessly dependent. Dr Wood began meeting with me on a weekly basis at the local general hospital where he would ask questions that never seemed to make any particular sense, whilst never proposing anything that might change my behaviour and feelings. Every week I returned and if he didn't ask me any questions, I sat there in silence. This caused me enormous discomfort and confusion and I wondered why we 'wasted' an hour's appointment on a regular basis like this. I didn't know where my problems stemmed from anymore. If he was waiting for me to talk, where did I start? As far as I was aware, my predicament was caused by my eating disorder and I couldn't understand why he wasn't attempting to tackle that, as I saw it.

I lived my life from one appointment to the next, as if they were a goal to aim for, the only one I had. Maybe it was because nobody had ever listened to me before, or because I was so desperate for a father figure in my life, or for someone to take responsibility for me, but my whole life revolved around those appointments and kept me going, despite the fact that my anorectic behaviour was not changed in the slightest.

A report from him to Dr Marks at the time read as follows:

"Dear Dr Marks,

Thank you for referring this young woman, whom I saw the same day at the out-patient clinic, 17 June 1985. I have seen her again on four further occasions, the last being with her husband. I should note at the outset of this summary that the conclusions in it do not at present add up to clear lines of progress forward. It summarises for the record various aspects of her history, at a time when she will be seen by my Registrar while I am on leave.

She is a daunting prospect in treatment for a number of reasons; in summary these reasons are the rigid pattern of weight control she exhibits, the long standing pattern of eating disturbance, the overlapping of eating disturbance with other behavioural disturbance and family conflict and, finally, the fact of her having carried her eating disturbance into engagement and marriage.

As indicated, she has a very tight pattern of weight control. She exerts tight control over what she eats but eats so little that she is readily prone to fatigue, powerful hunger and a sense of being unable to maintain control. If she eats anything approaching a normal meal she feels gorged and fearful of weight gain, but still very hungry. On some occasions she vomits immediately but on other occasions this feeling leads to her bingeing severely, followed by severe vomiting, which exhausts her and causes physical pain.

At the present time it is difficult to see where this pattern of behaviour can be altered through any agreements or contracts with her. Further, it is linked into other aspects of eating. In a normal routine she never sits down with her husband to have a normal meal; on the special occasions when she does, this is followed by the sense of engorgement and vomiting. She takes time to cook for her husband, including cooking him special cakes. During this cooking she may begin nibbling going on to binge severely. She eats a portion of his meal but does not serve any meal for herself. The food that is hence acknowledged as 'hers' is a careful low calorie snack diet.

As part of her contact with me in treatment she has agreed to keep a careful diary of her food intake, vomiting pattern and weight, which she has kept very carefully; as well she has agreed to note down her views and feelings during each day, a task she has again worked at carefully, clearly illustrating the inter-reaction between her weight and eating problems on the one hand, and her view of herself on the other.

Her eating disturbance began when she was 14 and she can date it precisely to a time when she was jealous of a group of girls who were sociable and successful and who were beginning to have boyfriends. At this time she felt overweight and wished to diet to become acceptable to them. After an initial attempt at dieting, she felt it to be too difficult and 'stopped eating', losing weight steeply. In her efforts to maintain a low weight, her sense of engorgement and fear of gaining weight led to her vomiting, which she utilised as a form of weight control. Bingeing began gradually two years ago and part of her present acute stress is a feeling that this is now out of control.

The pattern of eating disturbance in the interests of weight control has hence been firmly tied to her own desires about acceptable weight from the outset, in spite of there being a number of other events occurring at the same time. At the same time, there was disruption in her parents' marriage (see below). As well, Beverley in the same year moved from the top of her class academically to the bottom. In discussion, however, none of these other events link to her disturbance of weight control, in the sense of providing any other way of looking at the issue of her views of herself.

As indicated, there are issues in the family that it is tempting to link to her disturbance. She is the eldest of two girls with a sister twenty months younger. Her parents' marriage broke up when she was 14 after a relationship her mother had maintained with another man for three years. Beverley says that she does not recall having known about this relationship until she became increasingly suspicious and confronted her mother when aged 14. She and her mother left to live with this man but the relationship broke up five months later when he returned to his own wife. She recalls her mother seeking to blame her father, so that she had little contact with him (seeing him each two years), although contact has been closer recently. He has subsequently remarried.

At the time of the break up of the extra–marital relationship noted above, her mother was 'having a nervous breakdown' and she gives a convincing picture of drunkenness and drug overdoses, so that Beverley felt that she was 'leaning on me'. Subsequently, Beverley showed not only the anorexic pattern described above but also similar behavioural disturbance, so that between 16 years and 19 years she was taking overdoses and cutting her wrists. She met her husband at this time and it was at his insistence, she says, that she precipitately left her mother's home when 17 to go and live with him. In the meeting with them both, he commented that he felt he should stick with her in spite of her disturbed behaviour, since if they had not seen it through, the disturbance would have transferred itself into another relationship.

Beverley understands this disturbance in herself as part of her uncertainty, shyness and being prone to easily losing control (in contrast to her sister). Obviously at the time she would necessarily have come across to the outside observer as being powerless and suppressed. As indicated, her behavioural disturbance outside the area of weight control has settled in the context of the relationship with her husband.

The couple have now been married a year, a step they took after 2½ years engagement because of their commitment to a house bought. He is a successful draughtsman, slightly older than herself (I have failed to record his exact age). As part of his success at work he is now working very long hours (getting up at 5 a.m. and getting home at 8 p.m.). She describes him as having been confident and assertive but says his personality has shifted towards diffidence and shyness. He weighs only 9½ stone, half a stone more than when they met. She describes him as very fussy about food and also very easily satisfied after eating small amounts (so that, automatically, he does not eat much of the food she prepares him specially). In the only combined interview I have had with them, her own disturbance dominated the discussion and I have not taken up any of these issues of the interaction between their attitudes to eating and food with him.

She regards the relationship with him as a close one and they were mutually supportive and warm to each other in interview. Overall, in talking about the personal areas of her life, she finds some difficulty in putting her feelings into words, or is easily overwhelmed by the task of trying to. Her strongest feelings emerge in her diary and relate to her distress about the particular situation of her eating and weight difficulties.

Her course in treatment to date is implied by the comments above. Hence she has been able to give a detailed factual history, and there has been discussion about various aspects of the pattern of her weight control, although this has not led to clear conclusions about how she might feel more effectively in control of herself. In the other areas of her life it has not been possible to make clear connections between these areas and her weight difficulties, not surprisingly given the long-standing pattern of weight preoccupation. Beverley has shown a clear wish for support and guidance; as indicated, she has cooperated in the tasks I have asked her to carry out, in recording her observations about her behaviour and feelings. She describes herself as helped by the out-patient interviews, but only for a few days (in the sense of feeling more able to cope and less distressed about herself).

I apologise for the length of this summary, which is, in part, intended to record various aspects of her history. I will let you know of further progress.

Best wishes.

Yours sincerely

Dr A J Wood
Consultant Psychiatrist."

Dr Wood enquired as to whether I'd taken laxatives at such frequent intervals to the point that I began to think there must be some benefit to be gained from taking them if others were obviously doing it. Little was I to realise how hopelessly addicted I was going to become to those dreadful pills. Sometimes I dreamt of mountainous piles of shiny white tablets and even the mere thought of them became enough to make me sick. Before long I was taking 135 laxatives a day and getting huge satisfaction in watching my body visibly dehydrate so rapidly that the weight loss was actually apparent within hours. As the weight loss was only fluid loss and regained once fluid was replaced, the only way to keep the weight down was to continue taking them.

Laxative addiction is a dangerous addiction because it causes severe electrolyte imbalances, such as low potassium levels, that can cause a heart attack. Dr Wood didn't tell me this before I became addicted and it was impossible to stop them once I saw what they achieved; although as I was intent on causing as much damage to my body as possible, it probably wouldn't have made any difference knowing. With the size and quantity of binges ever increasing, as was my laxative addiction, it wasn't long before Dr Wood was carefully steering me towards accepting in-patient treatment. Eventually I relented, desperate to find freedom from the damn pills and bingeing.

Freedom however was not what I found inside the confines of the psychiatric hospital.

Annabel knew techniques that I didn't for losing weight and although I wasn't aware what she was doing at first, it didn't take me long to work it out. I became aware of the fact that she was swallowing copious amounts of pills throughout the course of the day. When she realised that I had seen her, she threatened me if I reported it. She grew paler as each day wore on and one night I went to bed heavy hearted, fearing for her life. When she surfaced the following morning it was quite a relief, which rapidly turned to alarm and disappointment however as I watched her consume more of the pills. As I watched her pitifully thin body twitching, I couldn't bear the burden of knowing any longer and had to tell.

The other patients made life particularly stressful, and no less stressful than life at home, just a different type of stress. 'Animal', as I named him, rampaged up and down the corridors hurtling abuse in all directions. Several times he had come to my bed and tried to molest me, or had pinned me against the walls in the corridors, asking for a kiss. I became terrified of bumping into him. Jim had the most horrendous scars on his forearm and was completely manic. Steve was a medical student whose wife had left him and he was perpetually morose and suicidal. Lucy had a baby and was depressed. These were the ones you could talk to, others sat in chairs around the dayroom from one end of the day to the other with their tongues protruding from their mouths, their faces contorting in awkward, ugly spasms from the lifetime of anti-psychotic medication they had been given. Confused arguments and paranoia were commonplace.

"What kind of a place is this for a nineteen year old?" asked Nanette as she left in tears, with dad adding, "I thought you'd grown out of this years ago!" And, "We'll get you out of here and see if we can find somewhere private, if Danny is in agreement?" Danny was in agreement, but it never materialised.

Both my parents were interviewed the moment they arrived at the hospital to visit and more than twenty years later when I obtained copies of my hospital notes, I was able to read for myself what was said during those interviews.

"Interview with Father at JRH, 14 October 1985

Mr Webber did not impress as unduly anxious about patient and was not happy with her admission, which he feels might have arisen because her husband finds her management difficult at home. He was critical of hospital arrangements concerning food and at the end of the interview I asked Sister to explain the treatment program fully. He sees himself as a religious man, concerned with spirituality rather than dogma and as practising his particular creed in his daily life. This does include being in touch with spirits, not necessarily ritualistically but more as an accepted and ongoing pattern. My impression was that he might be very firm about his views but his presentation was gentle and he expressed regrets about feeling he 'absented' Beverley after the divorce. There has, he feels, been better communication between them since and a better understanding on this point. He never felt she was alarmed in any way by the spiritual accentuation in the home when she was a child. Beverley goes to orthodox church. The family background is well documented in the medical record. There is one sister, Louisa, now 18, living with mother.

Childhood: Schooling:

Healthy, normal but had temper tantrums and did not sleep well, could not bear to be left. He remembers her as a loved and favourite child. No worries about food. Mother had occasional bouts of dieting. No particular association with grandmothers, though he sees his own mother as dominant and the maternal grandmother lived with the family for some time. Sees no problems at school, had friends, worked hard until she became 'overweight' at about 14. Parents did not know that she was vomiting after eating in order to lose weight until alerted by a teacher that she was not eating at all at school. She left school without qualifications — 'lost interest'. Not talented at anything, would like to be a singer in a band or creative.

<u>Parents Marriage:</u>

It was never what he'd really wanted physically but the couple got on well and he was surprised to learn of his wife's affair. He denied having affairs himself. He had known for some time before Beverley told him of her suspicions, and Beverley was extremely unhappy about the break up, and father blames the development of her illness on the split up in the marriage. She 'went haywire', went in for a good time, had affairs, etc.

<u>Divorce:</u>

He divorced wife when Beverley was 15, and is now married for 2+ years and very happy with Nanette, who is of Italian extraction, slim and warmly affectionate. She is also fond of Beverley and has helped her before. At first, however, Beverley stayed with her mother and Louisa lived with Nanette and himself, and Nanette's children, for a short time but there were difficulties, jealousies etc and she went back to her mother.

Prior to the divorce he had noticed Beverley developing 'puppy fat'. He did not think she was worried or he would have encouraged her to slim. She is 'well built'. Feels she may well have later envied Nanette her figure and indicated that she might have felt in need to be something like the woman her father wanted (my impression was that he had learned about this since that time rather than feeling it then). He settled into his new life without Beverley and since then has only second hand knowledge of her illness. Indeed, he had thought she was improving over the last year — 'it should have been upsetting, but somehow it wasn't'. He was 'disappointed for her'. He thought both girls should have elected to stay with their mother, who has not remarried and has been deeply unhappy 'like a zombie' for three years.

Drugs and Drinking:

Possibly one episode of drug taking. No problem with alcohol to his knowledge. Neither he nor his wife drink to excess.

Patient's Marriage to Danny:

They seemed very happy at first. He thought nobody had told Danny about the anorexia. Danny worries about money if they do what she lately wants, i.e. buy a house.

Father's Present Feelings:

'I handled it badly — she didn't contact me but I should have contacted her when we had split up.' In the last few months he has been in touch and been more demonstrative and open about his feelings. So far he has not had much response but feels it will come.

Summary:

Father's history of events reflected his early denial of guilt and ended with description of trying to re-contact and put things right — perhaps indicative of his new found happiness and openly expressed feelings. Nevertheless, I am unsure how much he really forgives anyone, and certainly feels he has a right to what he has now found and in the difficult early period described telling Beverley to 'say it's alright with Nanette even if it isn't really' (because it should be? — given his beliefs). Hence, due to this attitude and her sexually promiscuous history, plus mother's affair, trust will be very difficult for her in either male or female figures."

"Interview with Mother at DGH, 17 October 1985

Miss Frant is a plumpish lady who looked (and sounded when I telephoned her) very unhappy. In summary, she had an affair which eventually ended her second marriage and did not fulfil itself; her daughters cannot get on together, though Louisa still lives at home and she has had six years of intense worry about patient, with whom she has totally 'given up'. Her view is that everyone 'gives up' on patient and that Danny, like she herself, accedes to her every wish because of the ensuing tantrums and threats if they stand firm. Hence, that evening, each of them had telephoned estate agents for details of houses which neither feel the couple can afford because Beverley 'made them'. She is also persuaded that patient 'was best to leave hospital as it was not right for her.'

Personality of Patient:

She described Beverley as always introverted, very possessive and jealous of Louisa, very popular at school, clever, 'having a rich imagination', dominating, especially with Danny. Now like her father in that 'she never owns up to anything.' Avidly interested in TV programs on anorexia, 'wants to be a "real" one, wants a career of real interest. Basically shy, anxious, e.g. of telephones, hides under her make-up. Over protected by mother herself and her father.

Childhood:

Normal pregnancy and birth. A troublesome baby, crying a lot, bad sleeper until 11 months, a time when she also began to walk. Mother became upset through lack of sleep herself and needed medical help.

Ate well, never allowed to leave food and mother would induce her to eat a first course by sprinkling sugar on it. There were no scenes, she always then ate as directed. (Louisa made much more fuss.) Louisa also hospitalised early with skin troubles and tonsillectomy. Patient very attention seeking, very, very jealous of new baby who was born when she was 20 months and whose arrival mother had dreaded, fearing inability to cope with two children so young. Patient subsequently resented having to accompany mother to hospital to visit Louisa and got very bored there.

Mother's view is that she gave Beverley far more attention, because she demanded it, than Louisa. She also expected Louisa to be the jealous one and sees it as unnatural in Beverley. She then became very much attached to mother, screaming if she was left, e.g. at dancing class aged 3, at school later. Mother always met her and she screamed if this did not happen promptly. Improvement noticed when Louisa began school as Beverley took on role of protective elder sister. Louisa did not get on well at school, is described as unpopular and much less bright than Beverley, and often compared unfavourably with her by teachers. The sisters have never got on well at home. Louisa is 5 ft 2 ins weighs 8 ½ stone and is described as 'chunky'.

Events Leading up to Divorce:

Mother does not think there was any suspicion of her affair by Beverley. There were no rows, no arguments. She was surprised when alerted by her teacher that she was not eating at school. She realised that Beverley had lost interest in schoolwork but blamed 'music and boys'. 'She took money for school lunches, did not have them, then did not eat in the evening, saying she had had lunch.' Her husband knew of the affair from the start but did not want a divorce until he met Nanette. Mother cannot remember how the children were told of the impending divorce or by whom.

The Divorce and Subsequent Events:

Mother does think the actuality of the family break up affected patient, and she 'went off' her father and did not really have contact until over the last two years. She had been having feelings against father's religion for some time prior to the split, was confirmed C of E at 14 and disagreed with father's very firm (and in mother's view, pushing and domineering) views on religion. When father would ask 'What would Jesus have done?' in a problem situation, she became impatient and 'preferred common sense'.

Pattern of Family Eating:

Mother: An unsuccessful dieter, weight watcher — gives up and decides she was meant to be plump.

Father: Believed meat to be bad for him. Consequently often had something different from everyone else: he did eat chicken and fish. Mother therefore often cooked separate meals, first for her father only, then for them both.   Father favoured health foods, Beverley had vegetarian if possible.

Sexual Information:

Beverley had an early fear that she was not her father's child and mother has taken her to Somerset House to 'prove' that she is her father's child, explaining times and dates to her. We did not discuss patient's promiscuous period, the blame for which is put on the divorce.   Mother believes Beverley now fears sterility and this newly expressed fear may lead to a change in her eating patterns.   Couple have seriously expressed a wish to have a baby 'which would help'. Mother has discouraged this idea.

Early Family Pattern:

Like father, mother thought all was basically good. She was a strict mother and father's criticism of this was that sometimes she should say 'yes' rather than 'no'.   Mother does not remember Father hitting the children, she herself sometimes did.

Mother remembers good family holidays, but Father and Beverley always together, swimming and running and getting on very well.

Beverley's Marriage:

Couple have been married 1¼ years. Mother feels they are in love. Danny is good and kind but not strong enough for Beverley who needs to be made to do things.

Overdoses:

Two at home: said to be because she is bored: no hospital admissions.

Summary and Aim:

Individual psychotherapy long term to rebuild basic trust. She needs to know what is 'real'."

No sooner had I returned home from the hospital than the bingeing started again. In fact, it started before I even got as far as home as I stopped to buy food ready for the next binge on the way. In the relative privacy of a multi-storey car park, on the top level, I started to eat with my fingers from an ice cream tub. With tears streaming down my face, I screamed, "Help me! Please God, help me!" Where was God, I questioned, because life just continued on as before?

I panicked over how I would cope until I couldn't bear the thought of it any longer and resorted to taking a large quantity of Aspirin.

"What have you done?" Danny demanded, as we stumbled out onto a street. With my head hung in shame, I confessed to taking the tablets. "Oh this is just too much!" During the initial consultation and examination at casualty by a junior doctor, he enquired, "Why did you do it, Beverley?"

"Because I have bulimia," I responded nervously.

"That's no reason to die!" he retorted. "There are people in here who can't do anything to save themselves who are going to die and bulimia is treatable!"

Looking at him with contempt, I thought to myself, "You have no idea, do you, of the hell I am going through?" He sent me to have a stomach wash-out.

Whilst the procedure was extremely unpleasant, the nurses were kind, telling jokes as they passed the tube down my throat, a male nurse apologising profusely as he did so. Something happened at that moment which I was unable to understand at the time but which would make much more sense in years to come. The scene played on my mind as I relived the experience over and over. There was a perverse form of satisfaction gained that was to entice me again in the future. Maybe it was the fact that I usually retained such tight control over my body and during the procedure my body was under the control of others, an unknown experience in this form. Maybe it was because I hated myself so much that being abused by somebody else seemed to be what I deserved and mirrored earlier memories and feelings. I'm not sure what it was but something had been stirred within me, something fascinating enough to cause me to even write a song about it!

Four weeks later as a consequence of bingeing and too much self-induced vomiting, my throat was too swollen to be sick. No matter what I did I could not get the food back up. In a state of hysterical fear and panic at the thought of food being digested and moving beyond my stomach, I swallowed another overdose of Aspirin. This time I knew how to get rid of it.

I went to a different casualty for fear of being recognised, to get my stomach washed out. Lying, I told them that I'd never done it before when questioned. This time the nurses had a different attitude, treating me with disrespect and scorn. They used a wider tube than at the other casualty department and forced it down with as much aggression as they could safely muster.

Whilst there was not the same satisfaction as before, it achieved what I'd wanted it to. I stuck to the same story as before, that I was suicidal as a consequence of my bulimia, because I couldn't possibly own up to using it as a desperate last measure for getting rid of food in my stomach. Besides which, it was far too shameful to own up to having eaten and not been successful at getting rid of it — although I had to bear the terrible shame of food coming back up the tube as they flushed my stomach contents out, but it was worth it to get rid of the food.

There was another precipitating factor not taken into account at the time. During the week leading up to this second overdose Dr Wood had asked me to write a 'Fear Schedule'. He asked me to think about things from my childhood that had frightened me and to write them down. I had started to write down some of the occult experiences I had encountered but found I couldn't do it and never completed it. Dr Wood never took it any further, while I made a conscious decision not to mention it again either.

♣

Mum, dad, Louisa and I were sitting together in front of the fire with the ouija board balancing on the nest of tables. I was scared but knew just how important this was to them, so buried that fear as much as possible, as far down as I could push it. We each had one finger resting on an upturned glass and we waited.

"Is there anybody with us tonight?" mum enquired.

We waited, the fear prickling and stabbing from within me. The anticipation of a response would surely make my heart stop, the pounding so heavy within my chest. But another part of me wanted to see what enthralled them so much, that I wanted to share it with them. I wanted so much for them to love me that I had to be brave.

The glass jerked into life and slid abruptly to the word 'YES'.

"Tell us your name!" mum commanded the spirit, with neither hesitation nor fear in her voice.

Again the glass came alive and with our arms and fingers stretching to maintain contact, it slid from one side of the board to the other, spelling out the name: 'A—N—D—R—E—W'.

I was merely an unwilling observer at this point. My finger remained connected to the glass but fear had severed my mind from my body. I was elsewhere, anywhere but there.

I was 10 years old, where could I go from there except deeper within myself? Louisa, who was eight at the time, wore a similar expression upon her face to the one I thought I was wearing. I could see the terror in her eyes, and blank resignation written all over her, even though she never spoke of it, ever.

"Are you *St* Andrew?" mum asked with marked excitement in the intonation of her voice.

The glass slid immediately to the word 'YES' again.

How honoured we were that *the* St Andrew wanted to communicate with us. Even more so, that he had obviously been watching us and knew that mum and dad were set on communicating with him. I thought that mum and dad must be very special if St Andrew visited them and talked to them like that. But we were not allowed to tell anyone because people would be jealous, they wouldn't understand, we were told. They wouldn't believe.

St Andrew talked to us for a while as mum wrote down the letters furiously while the glass swept across the board in rapid, almost aggressive strokes, spelling out whole sentences and conversations.

Later, I lay in my bed, hugging my knees to my chest and praying the Lord's Prayer. Over and over.

I gave hypnotherapy a try during this period but found it useless. I also went to London to one of my father's alternative medicine exhibitions where I listened to a lecture on regression therapy, delivered by a 'Buddhist High Priestess', as she called herself. It sounded familiar, resembling the Christos I had participated in as a child, only with the difference of bringing about healing. I was keen to give it a go so dad arranged it for me.

Danny and I were sent to a rather non-descript house in London, where a lady in her mid-thirties, dressed more like a hippie than a High Priestess, ushered us inside. Whilst Danny waited in a sitting room, I was led to a darkened back room and asked to lie on the doctors-style couch in the centre. Incense burned around the room while the woman began chanting, and then more alarmingly, began dancing around the room waving rattles.

Something was wrong; I knew that inside myself. I lay on that couch, terrified and repeating in my head over and over the Lord's Prayer.

"Our Father, who art in heaven, hallowed be thy name... Oh, help me, Lord!"

My soul was supposed to depart from my body, travel towards 'the great white light' and bring light back to areas of my body that I could identify as needing healing from up above myself. In my mind I was encouraged to remove pain and hurting areas, replacing them with the light that I had carried back. Instead, I felt my body was openly handed over to something sinister as torrential waves of pure evil surged through me from the feet up.

I'm not sure what type of High Priestess she really was but I didn't return for anymore of this 'healing'. What I had encountered added another layer of fear to all the others. What had happened in her room was unfortunately reproduced in my own room that night, when I again experienced the evil surging through my body.

♣

An event was to take place soon afterwards that had the potential of bringing me to my senses but all it succeeded in doing was highlighting just how desperate and determined I was to lose weight at all cost.

As was often the case, I drove Danny to the station for his early morning train, arriving before 6 a.m. in semi-darkness, the station still deserted. Danny made the quick and irritated decision that the train was not going to stop there on this particular morning, as was sometimes the case, and he would need to race on to Epsom to intercept it. We raced at high speed through the wet November roads where he just managed to catch the train he wanted before I turned the car around to head back to bed. I was barely five minutes away from the station, swinging the car around an awkward bend, when I drifted over to the other side of the road a bit too far. The next few moments happened too quickly to remember the details.

The headlamps of another vehicle were bearing down on me. I was going too fast and I was already struggling to negotiate the bend. Turning the steering wheel as hard as I could sent the car into a 90 degree skid, avoiding the lorry, but heading at breakneck speed into a tree.

Metal crumpled around me, wrapping itself around my leg; the driver's seat concertinaed into something unrecognisable, pushing me into the roof of the car, whilst my leg remained trapped within the metal of what had once been the door. I tried to move myself but it was hopeless. I had no feeling below the waist and wasn't aware of any pain either. Carefully I managed to put my hands under my bottom and lift myself up off the crushed seat, moving myself only a few inches across, but my leg remained trapped.

It was still dark and the road was otherwise deserted. The lorry failed to slow and had long since disappeared. In the silence I could hear hissing coming from the engine and steam was rising from where the bonnet had once been, now just mangled metal. I knew there were some houses a short distance away and so I screamed in the hope that somebody might hear me. But nobody came.

Gradually daylight began to flood the scene and a young guy eventually approached the carnage and came rushing to my assistance. Realising that I was completely lodged within the metal, unable to be dragged free, he flagged down a motorcyclist a few minutes later and asked him to locate a phone box and call for help.

An ambulance arrived, followed by the fire service and the police. People were by now trying to get to work and the traffic began to mount up behind the ugly scene. Large cutting implements sliced their way through the metal, eventually releasing my body into the awaiting ambulance. I knew there was something wrong now as I couldn't move and still had no feeling below the waist.

As the nurse cut through my silk pyjamas and the doctor examined me, they both exchanged very obvious looks of suspicion. I thought it was at my lack of clothing, as it was now mid morning and I was wearing pyjamas, although it's possible it was down to revealing my skeletal frame and knowing instantly that I was either anorectic or a drug addict. I never assumed that people suspected because in my mind I was overweight. I was shaking from the shock but amazingly, there wasn't a mark on me anywhere. As the doctor leant across me, he made no attempt to prevent me from hearing him say "Huh, it's all for show." Then, without providing me with a gown, they threw a blanket over me and sent me off on the trolley to the x-ray department naked. In front of the porter, the radiologist removed the blanket to perform the x-rays and was horrified to find they'd sent me down with no clothes on. It was extremely humiliating and I have no idea why they treated me like this.

It was the same, now rather sheepish-looking doctor, who informed me that I had a triple fracture of my pelvis. With obvious embarrassment, he told me it would be extremely painful and was going to take weeks to heal. He admitted me to a surgical ward whilst a consultant contemplated pinning my crushed pelvis. Danny was with me when I experienced sudden chest pain later that evening and he rushed outside for help. A nurse hurried back with him, and when she saw that it wasn't an emergency, she sent in another junior doctor to examine me while Danny waited outside.

"Where did you feel the pain?" "Can you describe it to me?" I tried to. "Does this make you feel better?" He started to touch me intimately. I turned my head away from him in humiliation, silenced by the act. A tear prickled my eye. Laughing, he turned to leave, telling Danny on the way out that the pain was probably a delayed reaction to the trauma.

Was it my state of undress when I'd arrived that had caused his behaviour? Did they think I was a prostitute, or something? Whatever he thought, I had been treated with disrespect since arrival and so something about me obviously said I deserved it. Maybe they thought the car accident was deliberate, but that didn't occur to me at the time.

The next fortnight was spent on my back in an orthopaedic ward as we waited for feeling to return to my legs. I barely ate during this period and being bed-bound gave me a break from bingeing as well as from laxatives, which was the only relief. As soon as I regained some feeling in my legs I was determined to walk and go home. Only being able to stand for relatively short periods with the use of a stick, gave me another opportunity to overcome my bingeing and laxative addiction, but I couldn't do it. We hadn't got a car anymore and therefore the only way of getting into town for laxatives was going to be on foot. And, regardless of the excruciating pain from vomiting, I rapidly returned to bingeing. The desire then for those laxatives, that I by then knew I couldn't live without, was so intense that I frequently made the agonizingly painful and slow journey into town for them.

Dr Wood visited me at home every week after the accident. I was spending so much time alone without distraction and I desperately wanted him to understand and to do something to take the thoughts away. I planned to take an overdose before one of his visits in the hope that it would force him into taking control of the situation and rescuing me because I couldn't bring myself to actually ask him for help.

Danny stayed home for this visit as he had become increasingly concerned about my condition. "You look disgusting! Your spine is sticking out and red and you look more like a dragon than a young woman. Why can't you see it?" he commented with revulsion written all over his face. I couldn't though because I was never thin enough. Paranoia had begun to return and I couldn't physically turn my back from Danny, even in sleep, in fear of being stabbed with a kitchen knife again. By the time Dr Wood arrived, I was agitated, pale and nauseous, having swallowed a load of paracetamol. Dr Wood wanted to discuss alternative treatment plans and the way forward; Danny was insistent that something had to be done; whilst I sat, unable to communicate any of the pain I wanted to express.

"Where do you see your treatment going from here?"

"I don't know!" I yelled, taking them both by surprise. "Why can't you give me some antidepressants?" I whined.

"Well, antidepressants have undesirable side-effects and can be dangerous if you are not well enough, as clearly you aren't right now." He persisted in asking questions that I refused to answer, preoccupied with the growing nausea I was feeling and the fact that I couldn't tell them what I'd done, and with frustration that I hadn't collapsed.

Dr Wood suddenly knelt down beside me to take my pulse. "What have you taken, Beverley?"

"Nothing... What do you want from me?" I eventually screamed.

Dr Wood left and my heart sank because I had so desperately wanted him to rescue me from this nightmare, but it signified total failure in my mind to give in and ask for help. That night I was violently sick every ten minutes. The terrible feeling lasted for three days before subsiding, preventing me from even thinking about bingeing. And there it was! The reason Annabel had been taking the pills.

It was obvious, I suppose, that once it dawned on me, I would become hopelessly addicted to anything, no matter how dangerous, if it offered some relief from bingeing and obsessive-compulsive thinking. Still Dr Wood took no action, despite all the messages I was giving out of needing to be rescued. Inside, I longed for freedom, for anyone to take it all away from me. But ask for help, I could not. This would be an admission of complete and utter failure.

But despite what I presented to him, it wasn't the starving or the bingeing that I needed rescuing from. I longed for freedom. Freedom from the past. Freedom from the memories. I needed to hold onto my obsession with my weight for all it was worth because without it I would have to face up to what was behind it. And there was no way on earth I was going back there.

♣

We were in the back room at Jan's (John the Baptist's) house. This is the room where my legs were severed by a guillotine. The curtains were drawn and we sat huddled around a coffee table with our fingers resting on a strange contraption they called a planchette. It looked a bit like an artist's paint palette but it had a hole where a pen was inserted instead of a thumb, the tip of which rested on a large sheet of paper underneath it.

It seemed more sophisticated than the ouija board because the spirits could write down their conversations for themselves and we could read them as they were spelt out. To me, it looked like nothing more than scribble and I couldn't make any sense of it. I couldn't make sense of the fear in my stomach either, fear that sat like vomit waiting to be retched up from where it lay. Stagnating, venomous fear.

"It's not mum's fault, it's the spirits. This is life, truth. She's just telling us how it is. But I don't like it. I can't be brave forever. I need to escape, run away from here, from all of this. I need to run as far away as possible and never come back to this place in my mind."

♣

I could focus on starving, focus on recording every mouthful I succumbed to, like I was failing something with each and every bite:

5:30: cup of tea, one bite of Danny's toast.
7:00: cup of tea
8:30: 1 sweet
11:30: cup of coffee, ½ a biscuit, 135 laxatives
12:00: 2 cups of tea
20:00: very tiny bit of Danny's left over dinner on his plate, cup of tea, small piece of red pepper, 20 paracetamol
22:00: cup of coffee

I recorded the binges because they demonstrated failure too. Vomiting was a futile attempt at ridding myself of the poison within me because I saw the poison as the food itself. I ate so much it hurt and it had to come back up. But I couldn't reach the real poison. That stayed put.

> *1 large bowl of cooked rice,*
> *half a cabbage, cooked with half an onion and mixed*
> *with 1 pint of gravy, (prepared at the beginning of the*
> *binge and left to cook whilst eating the rest),*
> *flour, butter and sugar (quickly mixed together, pressed*
> *flat and grilled for speed), eaten smothered in jam and*
> *sugar,*
> *1½ pints of custard,*
> *a packet of sweets,*
> *a bag of applies,*
> *7 Weetabix plus Shredded Wheat with 1 pint of milk,*
> *½ loaf of bread,*
> *biscuits,*
> *2 litre carton of ice-cream,*
> *1 ½ litres of coke,*
> *1 ½ litres of water.*

Sometimes I managed to avoid bingeing by merely chewing food, not swallowing any of the juices and spitting it all out into a bowl at the side. Every waking moment was filled with the misery of a total preoccupation with food and weight, nothing else. Another short episode in hospital was to follow with the sole purpose of giving my body a break from laxatives, bingeing, vomiting and painkillers. As soon as another anorectic was admitted, I was off, unable to cope with the competition - when you always have to be thinner than everyone else, it's impossible to risk gaining weight when another anorectic might continue to lose weight.

Dr Wood referred me to Professor Clarke in London at a leading hospital for eating disorders, who put me on his lengthy waiting list for admission. He told me that I had severe, chronic anorexia and would need to be admitted for several months, whereby I would have all the control taken away from me and given a 3000 calorie a day diet in order to reach my target weight. He told me I needed long-term in-patient treatment. I couldn't imagine ever relinquishing control to that extent by going to such a place.

One night, as I lay downstairs sobbing, as I often did, Danny stormed down the stairs, pushed his fist into my face and shouted menacingly at me, "Will you shut up, or I'll shut you up, for you!" I lay in fear as he retreated upstairs, before pulling a few things together into a bag and leaving at one in the morning.

As if by leaving him, I would leave everything else behind.

Chapter 7

Camels in Yateley

DANNY PLEADED with me to come home but I was so confused because when I was with him he clearly couldn't cope with the way I had become, and his way of dealing with it was not to come home. When he did come home he was abusive towards me. When I wasn't there however it was a different story and he wanted me back. I travelled backwards and forwards between him and mum, not knowing whether I was coming or going. He hated me one minute and loved me the next. I felt overwhelming emptiness with the desire to die growing ever stronger within me.

Mum was unable to cope with the pressure of my being at home with her, finding it particularly hard when I insisted on chewing and spitting out my food. There were many hysterical rows, particularly if I ever got caught at night in the act of bingeing, which resulted in furious outbreaks of temper where plates would be thrown and things broken. Like a pregnant woman, my body craved certain foods and despite the fact that I had never eaten it before developing anorexia, and much to my disgust, I developed an enormous craving for peanut butter. Mum would buy jars in the hope that I would eat it; then once alone, I would eat the entire contents with my fingers straight out of the jar before being sick. In frustration at her persistence in buying the product, I often threw the jar across the room so hard that the peanut butter would be filled with shards of crushed glass and so rendered inedible. Throwing it into the bin would have been useless as I ate from the bin if desperate enough, even eating dog biscuits and other disgusting things at times.

"You're doing all this to hurt me and what have I ever done to deserve it?" she yelled at me one night as her favourite hand-made pottery cat was smashed as a plate of food crashed into the fireplace. "I've tried my best to help you. I've given you a home and done everything I can and this is how you repay me!" She hated me bingeing at night and I hated her knowing — it was shameful to be seen eating because it showed lack of control on my part. "It's easy for you to dismiss this and walk away from it when you don't like it!" I screamed back at her. "I can't ever walk away from it."

Staying at my mum's meant no more home visits from Dr Wood or my community psychiatric nurse, Marjorie, as I was too far away. This meant travelling regularly by train to see them during the week as I couldn't cope with changing doctors. On one such visit, Dr Wood and I were actually managing to have a reasonable dialogue for a change before pain got the better of me and I couldn't continue.

I stopped mid-sentence, trying so hard for him not to see how much pain I was actually in, but holding onto my stomach protectively. "Does your stomach hurt, Beverley?" asked Dr Wood, realising that I was struggling. I had stopped mid-sentence yet again, trying not to wince. "Have you done anything on top of what you normally do that might be causing this pain?" he asked. I told him that I was still regularly abusing painkillers along with the laxatives, but nothing in addition to this.

His tone changed. "Do you realise that paracetamol causes liver damage and you could die?"

"I know they do, but I just don't care anymore. I've failed at everything all my life. I've even failed at losing more weight. I've had enough. I *want* to die." I pleaded with him.

"It depends on how you look at it as to whether you've failed or not. Do you think you need rescuing from this current situation, because the way you're going, you'll be dead before the bed comes up in London for you and you may never get that chance? Do you think it might be sensible to be in hospital while we await this bed in order to keep you alive? You know, it could be seen as entirely different and separate treatment from that in London, purely as a preventative measure? In fact, I could arrange for you to go to The Grove immediately if you want?" His voice had an urgency about it.

"You're not putting me in that nuthouse!" I retorted, angrily. The Grove was near to my old school and I had grown up listening to rumours of what went on in there. It was a huge sprawling Victorian hospital set in extensive grounds, with its own church bigger than most town centre churches, and a purpose-built secure unit, East House.

"Well, you are probably nuttier than most of the people in there, so I don't know what you're worrying about, frankly. You cannot choose where you want to go or whether it's up to your standards or not. The Grove happens to be in your current catchment area." He paused before adding, "When are you going to let go of the fact that you are no longer the little rich girl you once were?" His words smarted and were left hanging in the air, as if he had just stepped dangerously too close to crossing the line. I wouldn't accept his offer and returned home, hardly able to stand by then, let alone walk.

I could not pull myself together though and the following day I repeated the obligatory exercise of swallowing another huge dose of laxatives and paracetamol. By the time mum came in from work, I couldn't even get up and was in bed. I felt very sick and everything was spinning. "Do you want to see anybody? Shall I call your dad, or Danny?" she asked. I think she thought I was dying, as I hoped I was too, but I felt too ill to bother with seeing any of them. I had begun hallucinating, even seeing really crazy things like camels walking along the pavement outside the house. I was getting paranoid about being dragged off to the Grove so I didn't want them to know how bad it was or how scared I actually felt.

♣

As I lay in bed, nauseous and longing for oblivion to hurry up and take over, the tired drab furnishings began to fade, being replaced by the familiar and more elegant surroundings of Fernhill.

The group had gathered in the blue room and a young couple arrived with their baby. Daniel was wrapped in bandages but his sad little eyes were peering out; a tiny lost person within the desperately frail body of a baby boy.

They came each week with Daniel to meet with mum and dad and the others in the blue room but then the visits stopped as suddenly as they had started. Dad said Daniel wasn't meant to live.

I felt such loss for them, and such guilt. Why had they come to our house? What were they doing with him? Who told them about my mum and dad? I felt that someone must have given them some false hope of a miracle, but who on earth had told them they would find one in our house because there had been no miracle cures before then?

I felt unsettled by Daniel's visits but nobody spoke of Daniel ever again and the couple never returned.

"So much fear, sadness and emptiness that it's best to run away, to hide, never to come back here."

♣

I became convinced that Dr Wood was going to send people to Section me and drag me off to The Grove and so I refused to answer the telephone or the door. The slightest noise sent me into a panic, and I intercepted all the post before mum got home in case Dr Wood was trying to contact her and there was a conspiracy going on between them.

I listened in on the extension as I heard her phone Dr Wood, pleading with him to do something. "There must be something you can do?" she was almost hysterical herself as she asked.

"I know it's very distressing for you to see what she is doing to herself and if it causes her harm, then there are measures that can be taken. In the meantime, I believe it is imperative that she accepts treatment herself for it to be of any value." This was supposed to reassure her but instead it left her feeling as isolated as I did. How much more damage did he expect me to achieve before stepping in because I was in so much pain, physically and mentally. Some days were so bad that I couldn't get out of bed for pain and nausea but in many respects those days were a blessed relief because I could neither eat or drink and was therefore also unable to binge or take laxatives, both of which I hated with a passion.

Since the night I had left Danny I had slept with mum in her bed. Unbeknown to me, she often lay awake long into the night listening for my breathing to make sure I was still alive. On this particular night I couldn't settle because of the discomfort I was in and Louisa and mum made up the spare bed for me as mum needed to sleep. The following day I overdosed on twice the quantity of painkillers I normally took and went to bed praying for oblivion and death. But morning dawned and I was still alive.

"I'm so depressed — I'm still here — still lying in the spare room — being nothing. 'Nothing' cannot even die. Why am I still here? I even wrote a note saying sorry and goodbye but I am still here to see the fat — what do I have to do to die? I fail at EVERYTHING. I took all the tablets I had, I didn't have anymore and I didn't even sleep. I want to die so desperately. I'm never going back to see Dr Wood, Dr Marks, Marjorie or Professor Clarke — I can't let them see all this fat.

Why don't I die? Is it a miracle that I survived? Does God hate me so much not to take me? I kept praying yesterday to let me sleep forever, but not to let me go to hell, because I am already there. But he's left me in hell — is this justice...?"

Dr Wood had already made contact with a consultant at The Grove, seeing it as only a matter of time before I ended up there, Sectioned, or otherwise. Eventually I did ask him for help, to his relief, I'm sure. He confessed that he had felt like some kind of a king with an attractive young girl in front of him to cure, but as this had become less of a reality he had become despondent and disheartened. I was amazed by his candidness and felt a sense of achievement that I had not lost control.

I did not anticipate that the next year was to be spent in hospital, or of what hell lay ahead, or the fact that never again would I return home to Danny.

I was admitted to The Grove on Saturday 8 November 1986. I was the youngest on the ward and over that first weekend was greeted with comments like, "What a shame!", "Aah, isn't she lovely, so pretty!" and "Poor thing!" I managed to avoid eating all weekend despite a couple of patients pointing it out to staff. The Sister laughed it off, telling me they were merely giving me the weekend to settle in but come Monday, they would be coming down hard on me and the whips would be coming out. Frightened, but convinced I could outwit them, I waited for Monday.

Dr Lawton, my new consultant, arrived as predicted on Monday morning, his hair carefully coiffured, his hand never without a cigarette. In response to his questions I tried to re-tell bits of my life and describe my current condition. Arrogantly, dismissing everything, he announced that I would eat three meals a day the same as everybody else!

"But I haven't come here to eat!" I argued with him. "I've come here to deal with my depression and to stop taking painkillers and laxatives in preparation for going to London."

"I don't accept that you are depressed because you would have succeeded in killing yourself by now!" he announced, merely adding to my sense of failure. "Nobody can be depressed as a child for as long as you've reported and not managed to die!" he exclaimed haughtily.

Dr Lawton's own notes read:

> "10 November 1986: Patient presents as a resentful, petulant, immature woman. Eye contact is minimal, replies to questions grudging and monosyllabic and she seems to have little idea why she came to hospital.
>
> Left after an unproductive interview, returned later to say she came to hospital to break the habit of taking laxatives and paracetamol, and for treatment of her 'depression'.
>
> Plan:
>
> Small meals, under supervision — continuing for 1 hour after each. Should not be allowed out of her room.
> Visitors to be advised against bringing her gifts of food.
> Avoid frequent weighing.
> Observe for 'smuggled' laxatives and painkillers.
> Dothiepin 75mg nocte
> Chlorpromazine 25mg bd / 50mg nocte"

I took an instant dislike to him but I had come prepared for all eventualities. From then on I went into the dining room along with the other patients with a small sandwich bag hidden inside either a pocket or a handbag into which I discreetly placed the food from my mouth, managing successfully to starve for a further two weeks. The pressure of being caught greatly intensified and to compensate for this I gave up drinking any liquid too.

Charge-Nurse Henry returned following a short period of annual leave, clearly able to see the weight loss the others had not noticed. Whilst I denied it furiously, the matter was presented nevertheless to Dr Lawton at the next ward round.

"Well, what do you have to say — you've heard what Henry is saying? Are you losing weight?" Dr Lawton looked slightly nervous.

"Of course I'm not with all this food you're giving me. I'm terrified about gaining weight because of what you're making me do! I can't cope with this regime at all." I chose my words carefully because I wouldn't actually lie.

"Did you deliberately try to kill yourself when you crashed your car last year?" he interrogated.

"No, I lost concentration and everything went blank."

"Humph!"

With a supercilious nod of his head, he motioned to his coterie with an air of superiority, inviting further questions. Whether I lied or told the truth it would appear Dr Lawton wouldn't believe me, but if he thought I might have deliberately caused the accident then at least he was beginning to believe that I was depressed. The interrogation continued, led by the power-driven consultant who managed to make me feel more worthless with every passing comment.

As I lay on my bed a few minutes later I was approached by a black-haired, long-bearded, and woolly jumper clad doctor who had been in the ward round earlier. Dr Rushworth strode confidently up to my bed and with a big grin on his face said, "Beverley, we forgot to mention to you a few moments ago that we don't want you going into the dining room wearing anything with pockets, or carrying your handbag anymore." As my face fell, he about-turned and walked away. His face said, "Got you!" and thinking they had won, it was clear that he was delighted with himself.

I was trapped. For a moment or two I sat trying to work out how I was going to get out of eating the three meals a day and quickly realised that it was going to be impossible. In a state of extreme anxiety I searched for the Sister to explain that it really was impossible for me to eat. "I'll go home. You can discharge me if you want because I really can't do it!"

Dr Rushworth was called back and together they tried to bring me to some alternative agreement. I was rigidly sticking to no solids whatsoever, offering to drink a cup of Oxo three times a day as an alternative to their suggestion of build-up drinks - which I wasn't having under any circumstances. Eventually I managed to bring them down to offering three spoonfuls of anything at each meal with a drink. It was to be eaten in a room on my own with a nurse and I was not allowed to go to the bathroom for an hour after each meal.

We were only a week or so into the new regime when Danny rang the ward to say he was being rushed into hospital for emergency surgery, which sent me into a complete panic. Danny had never been ill before and I wanted to go with him. We had a dog and a cat at home to feed and what would happen to them? Dr Rushworth agreed to emergency leave so that I could go home with Danny.

Whilst helping Danny and taking care of the cat and the dog were important, so was the need to get out to binge and to take laxatives. In fact, it would be hard to say which was the greater need as the two were closely interwoven.

I sat beside Danny on the surgical ward all day until the nurses suggested that I went home for a rest because his operation was unlikely to take place before midnight. On leaving the hospital I drove straight to a McDonalds where I bought two milkshakes, two portions of chips and a Big Mac, as well as stopping to buy chocolate. Upon my return to the cottage, I proceeded to eat everything Danny had in the house before vomiting and taking 100 laxatives. The hospital rang to say that the operation was finally underway during this frenzy and whilst my head was spinning with thoughts about Danny and The Grove, eventually physical exhaustion got the better of me and I drifted off into a fitful sleep around four in the morning.

The doorbell woke me the following morning. Mum had arrived to take me back to see Danny, before returning me to The Grove, as arranged. I was shocked to see Danny lying pale in his bed, with a drip in his arm and a drain from the surgical wound. The operation, whilst successful, had been more complicated than anticipated. He tried to whisper to me about the details out of earshot of mum. I sat holding his hand for as long as mum would allow me, devastated by his appearance and the fact that I had to leave him.

Dr Rushworth was at the ward when we returned and as he rushed forwards to greet us, he enquired as to how things had gone. I cried inconsolably over how awful Danny had looked and that I had had to leave him there. Once mum had gone his questions turned from asking how Danny was, to how had I coped?

"What do you mean?" I asked him tearfully, and naïvely.

"Well, I mean quite simply, did you binge and have you taken any laxatives since you left here yesterday?"

He appeared to be sympathetic and caring and so, falling for this, I confessed. With the confession in the open and armed with what he was apparently waiting for, he insisted on weighing me. Since returning home I now knew that I had lost a further 10lbs since my admission weight and I was terrified of this being discovered, becoming completely hysterical in my refusal to be weighed. He was getting louder and more insistent, eventually calling Charge-Nurse Henry and another nurse and ordering them to keep me in a side-room until I agreed to get on the scales. Between them they went through my bags and belongings searching for laxatives, which they confiscated. As time drew on and I refused to back down, they eventually relented with the weighing but placed me under constant observation, which meant being followed everywhere I went. Unable to cope with this degree of monitoring, I ran straight out of the building into the grounds, feeling agitated by the entire situation.

The following day I was simply unable to comply with even the three teaspoons of food. I wanted to go out for a walk but they refused, saying that Dr Rushworth would be arriving soon to see me. On his arrival he asked Charge-Nurse Steve to accompany us to an interview room for a chat. In a raised voice, Dr Rushworth threatened, "You have been constantly manipulative, taking the three spoonfuls to extreme. You are refusing to be weighed and unless you start co-operating with me, you are going to be Sectioned!" Not believing he had any grounds to Section me, I still refused to budge, insisting that they were being unreasonable and expecting too much from me. We continued to argue about the quantity of food I would accept and the fact that he still wanted me to be weighed until, out of sheer frustration, he snapped, "That's it! I'm Sectioning you and that's the end of it! You're a risk to yourself as you overdosed when you were on leave."

"Laxatives aren't an overdose!" I argued, becoming frightened.

"100 laxatives is an overdose and could kill you! You have said that you have no will to live and so you are being Sectioned until you eat and gain weight and that's the end of it!"

"But I've been taking at least a hundred for ages and I haven't died yet," I pleaded. "I want to go home!"

"Tough!" and he turned abruptly to walk out of the room, slamming the door behind him.

Dr Rushworth's notes read:

> '28 November 1986: Pt refusing to eat, refusing to cooperate with ward program
> – took 100 laxatives while at home
> – has very little insight as to dangers of not eating
>
>   Section 5(2)
>
> – side room
> – restrict privileges
> – to earn privileges, e.g. make-up, by cooperating with regime.
>
> She should also have to stay in side room for toilet and use commode to avoid vomiting.
> – not to come out under any circumstances till weight up and regular food intake

– to encourage to make decisions re which type of food

To review Monday

1:1 obs'

He sent a female nurse to take me back to my bed, where I was told to change out of my clothes and into a nightie. She proceeded to pack all my belongings including the earrings I was wearing and the rings on my fingers, my clothes, washing things, make-up, diary and books into a bin bag, before leading me down a corridor to a small room. It was then that I realised that I had been set-up, probably from the moment they allowed me to go on leave to be with Danny, in the hope that I would do something like this. The room had been prepared for this outcome: within it were only a bed, a chair and a commode. There was no carpet, only bare boards, the window locked and covered with wooden shutters. My belongings were locked up elsewhere; there was nowhere to hide anything, and nothing to hide. "Lie down on the bed and rest," the nurse suggested as she sat herself down in the chair by the bed.

Rest! I had no idea they could Section me once I was inside the hospital as an informal patient already and I was terrified. As I lay there, I could hear a vague commotion in the corridor near to my room as an elderly man was trying to get into the male toilets. My nurse got up to investigate and the moment her back turned, I seized the opportunity and ran for all I was worth in the direction of the day room. I had made a couple of friends, Rob, a ginger-haired, Scottish heroin addict and Marion, a middle-aged manic-depressive, and I was determined to get to them.

As Rob turned the corner towards me, I rushed up to him whispering, "Ring mum, PLEASE! They've Sectioned me! You've got to help me. Tell her to come quickly. *Please!*" With a tear-streaked face, I managed to scribble mum's telephone number down onto a scrap of paper before pressing it into his palm as the nurse tore around the corner in hot pursuit. Not surprisingly, Rob watched on in alarm as I was led back to the room, having promised to do what he could.

I refused to eat, drink or take the medication once back in that room. I was told that I was on a punishment/reward programme whereby everything had been removed from me, even the privilege of using a toilet or having a normal wash. I would have no visitors, no clothes, no belongings whatsoever, and these would only be returned gradually as I began to eat. Meanwhile, the nurses would sit in the room 24 hours a day, taking it in turns in hourly shifts. I would have to use a commode and would be given a washing-up bowl of water to wash in their presence.

Angrily and very afraid, I told them, "You can't force me to eat like this. You don't understand. My life is already hell and you are just making it worse. This isn't going to make me eat! I won't do it!"

"It will work, Beverley, just give it a go. Nothing else has worked," one of the Sisters pleaded with me. She put a screen across my door with a sign on it that all the nurses were to fill in, recording everything I ate and drank — an input/output chart. Feeling so humiliated by it, I cried with Sister Andrea as she sat with her arms round me, begging her to give me my make-up back because I couldn't cope without it.

"Is this the thing that means the most to you, Beverley?" she questioned, calmly.

"Yes, yes. I will eat if you give it back please. I promise I will."

"Well, this will be the last thing you get back then. There aren't to be any compromises anymore, Beverley. If you want your make-up back, you will have to eat to get it!"

Andrea sounded so kind as she spoke these words but I felt pure hatred then towards her. Why couldn't she understand the emotional cruelty she was inflicting upon me, that they all were?

Nursing Record reads:

> '29 November 1986: Beverley is adamant that she will not participate in any programme if she remains on Section. She has refused all diet, fluids and meds. Nursed on 1:1 as per programme and Duty Medical Officer informed of situation.

> Whilst Sister was sitting on the bed it was discovered that she had all of her make-up hidden in the bed clothes. She became abusive when staff took it away.'

That evening when the night-staff came on duty the Night Sister came to see me in my room and explained more about what was happening. "You are on a 72-hour section while they assess you and come to a decision as to what to do next. Unless you cooperate now, you will not get out of here when the 72 hours have expired." As she spoke, she hugged me with genuine warmth, stroking my hair and allowing me to cry on her shoulder. She brought in a bowl of water for me to have a wash and even agreed to bring in my diary to write up, whisking it away again afterwards. One of her staff sat by the bed throughout the night with a blanket wrapped around her as I tried to sleep, although unable to shut out the thoughts and terrible anxiety I was feeling.

During the course of the following morning, a commotion started up just beyond the screen outside my door again. As the nurse on duty in my room peered around the screen, I jumped off the bed, thumping her in the chest as I pushed her aside. As she tried to grab at me she slipped and fell behind me. I wasn't aware of what happened as I was just intent on getting out of that room and escaping at all cost. I wasn't able to think beyond this, for instance where would I go in November in just a nightie, assuming I managed to get past all the nurses anyway? I didn't manage it. I was later informed that the nurse that I had pushed had injured her ankle so severely that she had been taken to casualty. She was subsequently off work for several weeks. Bizarrely, I couldn't remember her or what had happened, only what they told me had happened afterwards.

I wouldn't look at any of them in my room, nor talk to them. I lay facing the wall with my face turned away from them because I had no make-up, crying endlessly, silently. Most of them didn't seem to care anyway, turning up with a book or something to read, making no attempt to help me through the ordeal. Sister Andrea was different though — she talked. Throughout her hour shift with me, she pressurised me to the point of giving in to being weighed at last. Then to reward me, she offered a bath.

She led me to one of the huge hospital bathrooms where a bath awaited me, filled with about two inches of lukewarm water. She positioned herself on a chair halfway along the side of the bath, with her knees almost touching the edge as she motioned for me to get in. Light streamed through the windows as I sat in the water, my hair hanging forwards over my unmade-up face. And I cried.

"You're having a reward! What are you crying for?" she exclaimed, as if saying what a silly girl I was. But nobody weighed me; nobody had known my weight since I was fourteen. Nobody saw me without my clothes on, not mum, not even Danny. Not a soul had seen me without make-up since I was fifteen. I even reapplied it before going to bed, creeping out of it early every morning to put it on again before Danny woke. This wasn't a reward — it was another punishment. I felt so humiliated and degraded. I felt like 'nothing'. Nothing could possibly be worse than this, I thought.

One of the nurses subsequently told me that Sister Andrea had told them that every bone in my body stuck out. There was an element of sick satisfaction in this, whilst also feeling enormous shame because someone else had seen me without my clothes on.

The Night Sister hugged me again that evening as I cried endlessly into her arms. "Beverley, it looks as if they are going to Section you again at the end of the 72 hours and it's highly likely that it is going to be for six months. You must start eating and co-operating with them because it will only get worse."

"How can it get worse than this? They are being horrible to me and I feel worse than I did before. I just want to die. There's no hope at all."

"You mustn't let them hear you talking like this," she pleaded, as she turned my face towards hers to get my attention. "Would you like to see Rob? He's been asking after you, you know?"

As I nodded, she got one of the other nurses to fetch Rob in quietly.

Looking rather awkward, Rob was ushered into the room and sat beside me on my bed.

"Rob, a minute that's all, or we will all be shot!" the Sister remarked firmly, but with a smile and a twinkle in her eyes as she disappeared around the other side of the screen.

"How are you?" Rob questioned in his heavy Scottish brogue, already knowing the answer. "I rang your mum but they gave me such grief trying to find out what you had asked me to do. I wouldn't tell them though."

"What did mum say? Did you ask her to come and get me? I've got to get out of here, they're doing my head in and I can't stand much more of this!"

"No, no, she said she'd ring the ward and find out what's happening."

"Uhh!" I didn't want her to speak to *them* first. I just wanted her to come and get me.

Mum sat there by the side of the bed crying. "I knew you weren't eating all they said you were. When they told me how well you were doing, I just laughed to myself because I thought they really don't know you very well. I knew you wouldn't give in that easily." I smiled a half-smile at her. "I just knew you were getting rid of it somehow..." Charge-Nurse Henry took her away to talk in the office about the Mental Health Act and tried to calm her down, which was a bit of a relief as it had been stressful listening to mum crying and it didn't make for a particularly pleasant visit in the circumstances.

When I woke up the next day I changed my mind about not co-operating and decided that I had to get out and, if I were to stand any chance of getting off the Section then I would have to eat. I ate everything they brought into the room, trying hard to talk and be friendly with some of the nurses that came in, which delighted them. Whilst I wanted to get out more than anything, I decided that if they did re-Section me I would not bother trying anymore. My reward for this, another bath!

At 10 o'clock the following morning Dr Lawton, Sister Andrea and Ian came to my room for the review. The 72 hours were up. I couldn't remember much of what was said during that meeting because I was so nervous, other than the fact that I told them I would not cooperate if they kept me on the programme but would try to eat if they let me out and gave me my things back. "Come on, Beverley, we've heard it all before. This programme will work and this is the way it is staying. If you won't agree to do it on an informal basis then there is nothing else for me to do but to Section you again, I'm afraid," Dr Lawton insisted.

Suddenly Ian blurted out, "She told me she will leave if we don't give her her stuff back and let her out."

As I glared at him in disbelief, Dr Lawton sighed, "Beverley, that's it! I've made my decision and I'm placing you on a Section 2."

Once Dr Lawton had left with Andrea, leaving Ian and I alone in the room, I shouted at him: "What did you do that for?"

Shrugging his shoulders he muttered, "I'm only trying to do my job."

Within a few minutes Andrea came back to tell me that they were moving me to a different room. The new room was at the very end of the corridor and half the size of the original one, with only enough space for the chair wedged down the side of the bed. Again there was no carpet, only bare boards, and the windows had shutters across them preventing any light from getting in. It was extremely drab and miserable-looking. The room was separated from the rest of the ward by enormous iron gates, which they shut and locked once they had moved me to the other side of them. So I was now a prisoner as well and unable even to try to run away if the chance arose.

A local G.P. turned up to do an assessment at Dr Lawton's request, because Dr Marks was too far away to call in at short notice. Not looking too comfortable with the job in hand, he arrived at the entrance of my room complaining, "Can't we have some lights on in this place? I can't see a thing!"

"You'll have to ask Beverley because this is her room and she likes it dark," Andrea informed him.

He looked at me lying on the bed, totally unimpressed and looking as if he wanted to say how absurd the situation was. He raised his eyebrows at me expectantly, to which I responded, "No. I want the light off!" which didn't get us off to a very good start. I couldn't bear them to see me without any make-up so I preferred to stay in darkness. I had, by now, given up hope of getting out and so I lay on the bed, attempting to hide my unmade-up face, but answering his questions honestly.

"I'm afraid I agree with Dr Lawton, Beverley and I'm going to be signing the papers too," he confessed before putting his notes back in his briefcase and dismissing himself.

Not long afterwards, two social workers turned up to carry out an assessment, another necessary part in the process. They posed all the same questions to me that everybody else had. "What will you do if you leave here?" Well everybody knew the answer to this and it would have been pointless trying to tell them I was going to enrol at college, get a degree and a career because they would have seen straight through it! I replied simply with the truth, "I'll go back into starvation," which was what I honestly wanted more than anything at that moment.

"What about the future, Beverley?"

"There is no future! All I want is to die."

"I think we'll just go and have a little chat with Sister Sam and we'll come back in a minute to see you again. Okay?"

Both of them got up to leave as I nodded, extremely frightened and feeling utterly without hope because I knew what was coming.

A little while later they returned. "Beverley we think you are very ill and need control taken away from you for the moment. Left to your own devices we believe you will die and so we will be signing the necessary paperwork as well." They left. What was the point? I refused to eat, drink or take the medication from then on.

"You've reduced me to nothing!" I spat at them. "This isn't going to work because you're only making it worse. You don't understand!"

Dr Lawton's notes read:

> '1 December 1986: This morning she sits in a corner refusing to make any eye contact. Manner is sullen but she converses reluctantly. Still childishly defiant. Has cooperated with program and privileges are being rapidly restored. She admits, of course, that she is eating only to regain the status quo and

announces her intention to resume her starving and bingeing as soon as she gets out of hospital.

During the last few days she has binged, vomited and taken an overdose of 100 laxatives.

Mother has been upset at the limits imposed on her visiting times.   Patient has not asked to contact husband since his operation.

Check with next of kin (husband) before deciding on Section 2…patient refuses to make a decision on whether to cooperate with program as an informal patient or force the issue.

Check with AMH re pending admission.'

The Section paper itself read:

"Joint Medical Recommendation for admission for assessment.

We (*full names and addresses of both medical practitioners*)… registered medical practitioners, recommend that…*(name and address of patient)*…. be admitted to a hospital for assessment in accordance with Part II of the Mental Health Act 1983.

I, …*N Lawton* … last examined this patient on: *1 December 1986*…

I had previous acquaintance with the patient before I conducted the examination.

I have been approved by the Secretary of State under Section 12 of the Act as having special experience in the diagnosis or treatment of mental disorder.

I, (*name of second practitioner*) ... last examined this patient on: *1 December 1986.*

We are of the opinion that this patient is suffering from mental disorder of a nature or degree which warrants the detention of the patient in a hospital for assessment.

AND

That this patient ought to be so detained in the interests of the patient's own health and safety.

AND

That informal admission is not appropriate in the circumstances of this case for the following reasons:

"The patient is suffering from anorexia–bulimia. She is uncooperative with treatment, repeatedly protests that she hates life and wishes to die, she has taken an overdose of 100 purgative tablets a few days ago and when she binges, the amount consumed is so great as to make rupture of the stomach a possibility."

Signed ...*N Lawton*.................... Date: 1/12/86

"She undoubtedly refuses to eat and will do so to her ultimate detriment — she doesn't care if she dies and says she has nothing to live for, and no long-term plans. She is mentally depressed. I feel she needs Section for her own survival."

Signed ...(GP)................. Date: *1/12/86"*

Nursing Record reads:

'1 December 1986: Continuous 1:1 obs maintained. No diet taken - very uncooperative.

Pt remains stubborn and protesting bitterly. Refused food and drink offered by nursing staff. Treatment programme discussed with Clinical Nurse Manager who advised nursing staff that pt must be reviewed by a doctor every day.

2 December 1986: (am) - To continue with present programme for time being. Continuous obs maintained on 1:1 basis. No diet taken, fluids taken. Ventilating her feelings towards the present regime she is on. Still feels like absconding and not cooperating.

(pm) - Treatment regime of reward system discussed with pt. Beverley resents this and feels that we are asking too much. Taken small amount of salad and fluid then complained about feeling depressed and wanting to die. Ran out of the room and refused to return, screaming and extremely disturbed.'

The Section was to last for twenty-eight days, five of which passed in that room and I no longer cared what happened or what they did to me anymore. The desire to die was a burning passion within me that never went away. I saw death as my only escape — from this, from anorexia, from life. I got so used to the routine and of having nothing, I no longer cared whether they gave me anything back because I knew I couldn't eat.

"If they hear you talking like this it will only get worse for you," Sister Sam insisted.

"How can it possibly get worse than this? I feel as if I am already dead and in hell!" I complained.

"Oh, it can get much worse, believe me. They'll transfer you to East House if you don't change your way of thinking!" she informed me. "Dr Lawton is only giving you two more days at the end of which we're going to start tube-feeding. I think we need to knock the fight right out of you and lower your resistance by increasing your medication."

I looked at her horrified. I was trying so hard to maintain what little control I had left. What would happen if they sedated me to the point where I didn't care what I weighed? I'd get fat and one day I'd come off the drugs and then I would see what they'd done to me and it would start all over again because I'd want to die even more.

"Beverley, I promise to make this programme more rewarding for you, if you will only begin to make an effort to cooperate with me," begged Dr Lawton. "Professor Clarke says that he's very disappointed we've had to resort to such measures with you, but we didn't have a choice. He told me that the bed in London will be available soon. There has been a delay while they have been redecorating the ward apparently but it shouldn't be too long now, any day in fact." He paused before going on, "Beverley, I agree with Sister and am going to double your medication and will begin tube-feeding tomorrow if you don't start eating today."

Dr Lawton's notes read:

> '3 December 1986: Long interview – alone. Much more communicative. Accepts that she forced the decision on Sec 2 and seems untroubled by it. She does however feel humiliated by the programme of progressive rewards but accepts that her being treated as a child is the inevitable outcome of her childlike behaviour.

Still feels her basic problems are 'depression', feelings of inferiority, inability to communicate.

Agrees to try again to cooperate

Programme: bring forward use of bathroom.'

Tube-feeding had always been my biggest fear as it meant total loss of control and there was no way I would allow that to happen. I gave in and picked at the food they brought in. I was so drugged up that I slept a large proportion of the time in the room, being woken up only for the food. My 22nd birthday was days away and I felt particularly depressed at the thought of spending it alone shut in that room.

"You're lucky to be alive for your 22nd birthday, frankly!" Sister Sam remarked.

"Oh, don't be so stupid! I've been like this for years and nothing's changed!" I laughed.

"No, I'm serious actually, Beverley. Dr Lawton said you could have died any day before we started this programme."

I just looked at her, speechless. Was I really as ill as she said? I didn't believe them because in my mind I was still too fat and wanted to lose more weight.

I began chatting more to the nurses as they sat with me, although some always came with a book and I knew not to talk to them. As I ate over the next few days more of my belongings were gradually returned, including my make-up. Once I got that back on my face I allowed them to switch the light on again and open the shutters. It felt nice to be in the light again as it had been dark for so long. I learnt to keep my feelings to myself because inside I was screaming even louder, ever more despondent with each passing day, wanting to die an inconsolable fervour. Anxiety was mounting as I faced the reality of weight gain being inevitable. My objectives were simple: stay in control as much as possible, prevent tube-feeding, get out of the room, return to starvation as soon as possible — die.

Dr Lawton's notes read:

> '8 December 1986: Continues to improve — privileges being steadily increased and she is happy with this. Still maintains that she feels depressed most of the time and has no interest in continuing to live.
>
> Considerably reassured and encouraged by interviews but continues to maintain that she is depressed.
>
> Omit Dothiepin stat
>
> Start Nardil after 5 days.'

Despite the regime I still managed to fool them with food. They really had no idea when it came to dealing with an anorectic. Every morning when my breakfast came I asked to use the commode and the nurse would wait on the other side of the screen. With my shutters open and the window open an inch at the bottom, I would throw the toast out through the gap as quickly as I could. I always expected to get caught but it just didn't occur to them. As I sat on the bed one morning I noticed, with sheer horror, a squirrel running up the tree by my window with my piece of toast in its mouth! Looking away and trying to distract Ian with a conversation, he suddenly glanced up and noticed, "Hey! Just look at that!" he announced, with a hint of glee in his voice.   My heart was thumping; he would suspect, he's bound to, it's obvious… He didn't.

As the weeks passed in that room, I told them, "Food is life and to eat therefore means I accept life. I don't accept it and as long as I want to die, I cannot eat."

Monday 5 January 1987: *"Oh I feel very bad this morning. I have just an empty space inside — a big gap, meaning I am nothing again.   It's such a horrible feeling — the only feeling I have, other than feeling very fat — which is even worse today after what I ate last night, so I went straight out after breakfast for 60 laxatives.   I hate them but it is necessary when I am full of such self-hatred. Please take it away from me. Will these laxatives kill me? Why won't they? Why can't I die after all I do? By lunchtime I felt sick — so I ate a whole meal, (steak and kidney pie, two potatoes, carrots and three ice creams) then I was in so much pain. My stomach is so swollen and sore from the laxatives — I made myself sick.   I felt like death and spent the whole afternoon on my bed feeling ill."*

By then I was having my meals back in the dining room with the other patients, allowed off the ward occasionally but still spending time in-between in my room with a nurse after meals.   By the time tea arrived in the dining room on 5 January — after I'd written the above diary entry — I was feeling very sick and didn't know how I was going to face the next meal, having taken the laxatives earlier and already having been sick.   Reluctantly, I queued with the others, having to sit down in a chair because I had such severe stomach cramp. I was bent over double in pain and as I held onto my stomach, my breathing quickened. Beginning to panic as I wondered what was wrong with me, pins and needles started to spread along my fingers and arms; then my legs and feet also. As I grew more and more frightened my hands turned into stiff, rigid claw-like shapes that I couldn't move. My face began to twitch and I couldn't call for help because I discovered that the muscles in my tongue and throat had also been affected and I couldn't talk. I was convinced I had caused a serious chemical imbalance as a consequence of the laxatives I'd taken earlier and was about to have a heart attack. I was terrified. Andrea walked in.

Andrea swore. "Somebody call the duty doctor quickly!" she yelled. "Steve, help me!" As the two of them picked me up and started to carry me out of the room they talked over me, rather than to me: "She must be having some sort of reaction to her drugs, or something…"

Dr Webb ran around the corner towards us as Andrea and Steve were half carrying me, half dragging me along the floor. "In here, in here," one of them said as they kicked the door to a side room open. Dr Webb began to calm down almost immediately as he told me to sit in the chair opposite him. Andrea sat down as well as he started to talk, composed and smiling at me. He was asking me questions but I couldn't move my tongue to answer him. Why wasn't he doing something to help me? How could he just sit there being a stupid psychiatrist, asking questions, when there was obviously an emergency to deal with? But ask questions and talk in the same gentle, peaceful manner he continued to do. Gradually the muscles in my hands began to relax, ever so slightly. After several minutes he paused, "Beverley, I want you to walk back to your bed now and lie down and I'll come and see you in a minute. I just want to have a quick word with Andrea."

What was going on? As I started the journey back along the corridor I felt like I was in 'Alice and Wonderland'. I was clinging onto the walls in order to walk because the corridor seemed to stretch out before me like a long, distorted tunnel; sounds were echoey and seemed a million miles away. As I groped my way along the walls I was crying and screaming, not believing he was making me do this in this state. "HELP ME! HELP MEEE!" The screams seemed to come from somebody else. Eventually I made it onto my bed just as Dr Webb walked in and put his hand on mine: "You're going to be fine, it's okay." He was still smiling, which really irritated me by now because I didn't understand.

"I'm not fine at all!" I yelled at him.

"What you have just experienced is something called tetany, which is caused by low levels of potassium in the blood as a result of taking laxatives and by hyperventilating. You *will* be fine!" he reassured me.

Duty Doctor's notes read:

> '5 January 1987: I was called to see patient because of disturbed behaviour. The patient presented crying, hyperventilating and spasms with flexion of muscles of hands, adopting foetal position of body.
>
> Interviewed in office
>
> She sees herself as fat, ugly. The patient hates herself. Suicidal ideation present
>
> Management: Observation. Transfer to room where she can be observed.'

The programme continued unchanged. Generally I ate enough to be allowed time out of the room, but the sense of worthlessness and degradation I felt as a consequence of what I'd endured was enormous. I still abused laxatives when I got the opportunity to leave the ward and on one such trip, purchased razor blades as well. A couple of times in the past I had scratched at my skin with needles but I had kept these scratches concealed. Now I hated myself with a vengeance and I was hearing thoughts in my head urging me to cut myself that were driving me to distraction.

Dr Alikhan and one of the nurses held my arm up above my head in the treatment room to stop the blood flow. "You'll have to do better than this if you want to die!" Dr Alikhan snapped at me as she cleaned up the mess.

Duty Doctor's notes read:

> '8 January 1987: 1.30pm - Asked to see.
> Has slashed her L wrist using a razor blade. OE superficial wound 3 cm on L wrist. She said 'I felt very bad because I ate too much this morning'. Felt guilty because she ate too much and didn't vomit.'

> '12 January 1987: 9.20 am slashed her wrist again, creating a superficial wound 3 cm on L wrist. Doesn't give any explanation as to why she did this.'

Dr Lawton's notes read:

> '16 January 1987: Little change; she feels that wanting to be normal is a sufficient contribution from her.'

Chapter 8

Strange Little Girl

ON 5 FEBRUARY 1987, I was finally transferred from The Grove to the eating disorders unit in London. The Grove had certainly kept me alive, but at what cost? I was not at all prepared for what I found in London and any glimmer of hope there might have been at finding help there rapidly evaporated into thin air.

I was confined again 24 hours a day to a small room; more pleasant this time than at The Grove, with carpet, a chair, a table, and a wardrobe. I was even told that I could decorate the walls with my own pictures if I was interested. I wasn't. I was confined again, back to washing from a bowl they brought in twice a day and having to use a commode. On top of which there was the food — a 3000-calorie a day diet! Every single item on the tray had to be eaten because it had all been carefully measured out, even down to pots of sugar with the cereal and jugs of milk. Nothing could be left.

The entire length of my wall running alongside the inner ward corridor was one enormous expanse of glass. Other patients, staff and visitors walked about the ward on the other side of the window whilst the anorectics remained in their rooms, living lives more resembling that of goldfish. I felt like an animal in a cage being fattened up — and for what? I had no life to return to.

Twice a week I was weighed; being pushed down to the weighing room on my commode along with the other five anorectics on the same programme. I wasn't allowed to walk anywhere or use up any energy doing anything for myself, even down to making my own bed. Hour upon hour went by in that room on my own. The same feelings of worthlessness and hopelessness overwhelmed me, along with suffering terribly with sleepless nights as they'd withdrawn all the medication I'd been on at The Grove. I chucked as much of the food out of the window as I could, although with windows again that only opened an inch, it was near on impossible trying to chuck rhubarb crumble and custard out of it by the spoonful! Sometimes I just left the food on the tray despite knowing this would generate a fuss.

Within a week, I knew I wasn't going to be able to complete the programme. I was so traumatised by what had happened at The Grove and all I wanted to do was go back into starvation. I had simply given up. Having brought my supply of razor blades with me, that neither hospital had discovered, I lay on my bed cutting my wrist. The blood spread rapidly across my white nightie as I lay there with my arm across me, until it looked more as if I had been stabbed in the stomach. And I just lay there... and lay there. Nobody came and I wasn't allowed out of the room. It was some forty-five minutes later when somebody peered around the corner of my window and, instantly seeing the mess before her eyes, flew into a surreal, silent panic. The nurse sat me on the commode, threw a blanket over me to cover up the blood soaked nightie, and pushed me furiously down to the treatment room.

Dr Richards walked in.   He was extremely curt and unpleasant and proceeded to stitch up my arm immediately without any local anaesthetic or fuss. I refused to give him the satisfaction of reacting to the pain so I kept still, showed no emotion, said nothing and gritted my teeth. I was taken straight back to the room and told that nobody would talk to me in order to punish me for what I had done because I could not manipulate the situation to bring about more attention for myself by cutting. I would be spoken to as and when they dictated and not before. This seemed heartless and unnecessary. Why did they think the cut was to get attention when all I was trying to do was to stop the turmoil going on in my head? It had nothing to do with them!

I cried alone in that room after they'd left me. Why wouldn't they give me anything to cling to for hope? I wanted them to take away the thoughts first but repeatedly I was told that the treatment wouldn't start until I reached target weight. Surely something had to change first because where was the motivation going to come from when I had none? How could I trust them that it was going to feel better after the treatment?   Until then, eating generated extreme anxiety with my mind telling me that everything was terribly out of control.   To me, it seemed as if nobody really understood and all they were ever interested in were target weights.   They were simply reinforcing my sense of worthlessness by their actions. I couldn't trust them, just as I couldn't trust anyone else. One meal I would try to eat but would then be thrown into a terrible panic, so the next I left. My mind was in turmoil. Where were they then? It was apparent that I was completely on my own, as had always been the case.

Dad came to visit one evening, threatening me that if I refused to cooperate with the programme then he would have nothing more to do with me; he would disown me as his daughter! Hadn't that already happened several years earlier? I watched him in silence as he turned to leave and march back along the corridor to the exit. If there was anything to cling on to in order not to lose it, it would be worth fighting for but as I watched him go, I knew there wasn't. Dad had already walked out of my life several years earlier when he married Nanette, so losing him again wasn't going to make any difference.

Danny's words were even more menacing than my father's. "If you come out of here the way you went in, I'm leaving you!" It was spelt out with such hatred in his eyes, it seemed. I didn't care about Danny or our marriage any longer, and neither did he. What did it matter if he left me?

Professor Clarke spent the first two weeks of my admission on holiday and by the time he returned I had given up on the unit. "You know how miserable living with anorexia is and what returning to that life is going to be like. If you want help, then you have to agree to eat and reach target weight. How do you feel about this now?" he asked during ward round, surrounded by a number of people on his team.

"I don't want to return to the way I was living before, but I don't want to reach target weight either," I replied honestly.

"Does that mean you are not prepared to commit yourself to this programme?"

As I sat there with my head down, the whole room seemed to be sitting on the edge of their seats in silence, waiting for my response. I eventually managed one word, "No."

"I'm very sorry indeed to hear that, Beverley. I have no alternative but to discharge you now and make the necessary arrangements for your transfer back to your family and doctors at home."

Final Summary to GP reads as follows:

'Diagnosis: Anorexia Nervosa. Bulimic variant
Contributory Factors: Disturbed family background
Treatment: Full anorectic regime
Progress: Beverley initially refused to eat for the first ten days then made an attempt to start eating, but soon gave up and discharged herself.
Condition on discharge: Profoundly anorectic
Disposal: To GP and catchment area psychiatrist
Prognosis: Poor'

There seemed nothing for it then. I returned home. Danny left me. Nobody in the world seemed to care or understand. Life was unbearable and everything was a waste of time, there was nothing to get better for, nothing worth fighting for. There really was only one alternative left. I had to succeed this time with an overdose. I went back to bed one morning after swallowing 70 sleeping tablets. Having never overdosed on sleeping tablets before, I was sure that I had taken enough of something this time that would bring about an end.

♣

Are they going to come and knock on my wall like they do for mum? Mum says that her dad knocks on the bedroom wall every night. Ken was killed in the war when she was a child and he was her reason for getting involved in the occult in the first place because she longed to find him. But I didn't want him knocking on *my* wall. I wanted them all to go away. It was all his fault that mum and dad had got divorced. She wasn't meant to be with Fraser at all. He lied.

I want them to leave us alone. Leave *me* alone. I want to be like everyone else. I don't want to know anything about life after death, and what's really out there. I just want it all to go away.

♣

Through the fog of drugs I was suddenly aware of Glenda, my CPN, sitting on my bed. I reached out for her hand and she squeezed it tightly. "Let me go, Glenda. Please just stay with me and hold my hand…"

"You know I can't do that," she whispered, tears flowing down her own cheeks.

♣

Nursing Records read:

> '20 May 1987: (pm) − East House. Admitted this evening under Sec 2 of Mental Health Act.

Accompanied by Social Worker. Spoke in soft voice and said she could not remember what happened in Royal Surrey. Discharged from RSCH 48 hrs ago prior to admission. Stayed at CPN's home last night. (Nocte) - Observation maintained - very quiet. Temazepam 20 mg given with little effect. Keeps shouting and crying for her mother. Very little sleep.

21 May 1987: (am) - Waiting to transfer to Red Ward - keen to transfer as she appears very nervous. Curled up in chair and rarely venturing out of it - withdrawn and isolated. To remain on EH for a couple of days until vacancy arises on Red Ward.

(pm) - Mainly isolated herself - curled up in a chair. Refused to eat any solid food but will take tea (fluids). Very hysterical. Eventually led to a side room - Valium 10 mg intramuscular PRN given as instructed by Duty Medical Officer Dr Alikhan as Beverley screamed occasionally. She appeared tense and shaking.

(Nocte) - Remains isolated. Had her night medication but with very little effect - awake most of the night, sometimes screaming and calling for her mother.

22 May 1987: No outbursts of screaming - remains very quiet.

(Nocte) - Still isolates herself but a little more cooperative. Temazepam 20 mg given at 10 pm with very little effect. Very little sleep, walking around her room most of the night.

24 May 1987: (am) - Advised not to curl up in chair. Advised to eat breakfast which she refused - she is still negative about eating. Went out in grounds but did not stay long as she tried to climb over the fence twice. She was brought back in to ward. Not very communicative - she was asked if she would like to talk about problems and the way she feels but she said 'No. I want to shrink and die'. Later she asked if she could talk to me, I said yes but when she came in the office she said there is nothing to talk about. She sat for awhile and then left.

(pm) - Pt still feels life is not worth living. Pt continues to refuse to eat.

26 May 1987: Seen by Duty Medical Officer – to move to B Ward.

Moved to B Ward - oriented to the ward.

Pt noticed to be missing at approx 6pm. Beverley had gone to the toilet at approx 5.45pm and no indication was given to her leaving the ward. Duty Medical Officer informed - missing person form completed - local area was searched and the area around the hospital. Police informed - NOK informed - Stand-in Nursing Officer informed.

(Nocte) - Brought back to the ward by police at 10.06pm. Mood quiet and subdued. Duty Medical Officer informed who said to keep Beverley under discreet observation.

27 May 1987: Observed discreetly. Remains sullen and aloof curled up in a chair for most of the time.
Poorly   motivated   and   not   initiating   any conversation.
Seen by Records and her Section rights explained to her.
Minimal amounts of fluids taken today.

28 May 1987: (am) - She sat sullenly all morning and was reluctant to enter into any conversation. She answered questions but her answers were barely audible.

(pm) - Seen by Dr Lawton. Beverley appeared very meek, speaking in a low whisper that was almost inaudible. She was told very clearly and in no uncertain terms by Dr Lawton that she was behaving in a childish and extremely unsuitable manner and that it was up to her to make an effort to improve.'

Chapter 9

Dying To Be Free

THE ROOM WAS DARK and dingy; no lights and only one tiny window near the ceiling, which offered nothing of life outside. I had only minutes, perhaps just seconds, to achieve what I had run in there to do. Slamming and locking the cubicle door behind me, I sat down on the toilet and reached for the razor blade that I had hidden.

I began to cut frantically at my wrist. Tears were streaming down my face, but I felt no pain. As I cut through the first layers of skin, I came to the globules of fat that repulsed me, and which I fought to ignore. I had to work quickly because I knew that I would soon be missed from the day room and very swiftly located. Within seconds blood was pouring on to the floor and spreading out under the cubicle door, and as the blood flowed, I began to experience relief at last from all my anguish and torment. With the first cuts my mind was focused on the hatred I felt directed at myself, at all the frustration that nobody understood or cared. But even these feelings faded with the release of the blood. It was as if they too gushed from my body onto that dirty, blood-spattered floor. My thoughts were pushing me further towards death and I longed to find freedom. How long would freedom take to arrive? Had I cut deeply enough? I carried on just to make sure.

One of the nurses burst into the room and, swearing, ran back out again. A dreadful commotion ensued, with a doctor and several nurses carrying me out of the toilet, attempting to stop the blood flow as they waited for an ambulance to arrive. "Leave me alone!" I cried, longing for oblivion to take over.

"Shut up and do as you're told," rasped Dr Webb through gritted teeth.

At the general hospital I received emergency surgery under general anaesthetic, awakening the following day to my arm in bandaging and foam padding, suspended from a frame above me. I had survived, again. Four days earlier I had taken a large overdose of paracetamol and had been told that I had been lucky to survive. Lucky?! I was *trying* to die. Surviving was not what I considered to be lucky. Surviving meant I got sent back to East House under even stricter regimes than before.

East House flashed through my mind. It was a place full of tears and screaming; so full, it felt like the very walls would explode. Sometimes it felt as if I had lived there forever and that I would probably grow old there, it was so hopeless. And now I was going back.

When I awoke again I was in an empty cell, lying on the familiar red plastic mattress on the floor with my arm in a sling. Dr Lawton was sitting beside me alone for a change, and with a look of unexpected concern, he said, "I am extremely worried about you at the moment, Beverley, and under no circumstances will you be allowed to leave this hospital. I am going to place you under a further Section. How do you feel about that?" What did I care anymore what they did to me? Despite the pain I was in, the desire to die was as strong as ever. Everybody knew that if I left the hospital I would immediately go back to starving myself. I replied, saying, "I don't know what's happening to me. I haven't got any control over my thoughts. Something else is controlling me and I feel like I am cracking up into a million pieces." He nodded, telling me that he was increasing my medication, before leaving me on my own again.

Dr Lawton's notes read:

> '24 June 1987: Shortly after last interview yesterday afternoon, patient slashed her left forearm with a razor blade. She shows no evidence of clinical depression but her mental instability is such that she presents a real danger to herself. The nurses feel that they have no control over her as an informal patient.
>
> Detain Sec 3 if GP and Social Worker are in agreement
>
> Beverley accepts that this is yet another refusal to accept responsibility for her actions but at the moment I can see no practical alternative.'

That night the thoughts in my head were so fast and self-destructive that I became increasingly agitated. Those thoughts took hold of me. They were frantic and frightening. I was out of control, unable to fend off the onslaught of those compulsive thoughts. In sheer desperation and to bring about an end to the raging turmoil in my head, I began to rip the stitches out of my arm with my own teeth. I had no other means by which to mutilate my body and it felt as if I needed to tear myself apart to get rid of the thoughts. It was with utter frustration and hatred for the body that put me through such hell, that I was driven to punish it.

I was interrupted by two male nurses who unlocked my cell door and, while one of them held me down on the mattress, the other injected me with something. They were laughing and before leaving they tied my hands together with the bandages I had removed from my arm, in the hope of restraining me before I was knocked out by the injection. They retreated from the cell, locking the door behind them. The moment they had gone I started biting through the bandages, tearing them in half to release my hands. As soon as they were free, I tied the bandages around my neck and began to pull them tight, strangling myself. The door burst open and the same two nurses barged in, removed the bandages from my neck and this time held me down until darkness swept over me.

Nursing Record reads:

> '24 June 1987: Returned from RSCH with L forearm explored and sutured. Arm elevated and nursed in dressing gown. Will be seen by Dr Lawton - poss Sec 3 to be implemented.
>
> Nocte: Pt unable to settle down during the night - she is trying to kill herself by removing stitches to her arms. Duty Medical Officer informed about the behaviour and so PRN Largactil 100mg was prescribed and given about 12.30am by intramuscular injection. Obs maintained.'

The following morning I was so full of drugs I could barely walk. A nurse stayed behind to help me wash before leading me downstairs through a sequence of doors, pausing to unlock and then lock each one, before we arrived in the secure day room. I spent the day slipping in and out of sleep, unaware of the time or what was going on around me.

Dr Marks arrived mid-morning to interview me at the request of Dr Lawton, a formality required for the new Section to be enforced. Since I had been Sectioned several times before by then, I was well accustomed to the procedure. It meant that I would be detained by law for a specific period of time, depending upon the Section chosen by those interviewing, usually at the suggestion of the consultant in charge. As Dr Marks had sent me to the hospital on a Section 2 (which lasted for 28 days), after Glenda had summoned his help the day of the overdose, I could not be held under the same Section again. This meant I was facing a much more lengthy Section since the next step up, a Section 3, lasted for six months. Different aspects of mental illness would need to justify the longer term involved and it also meant that treatment could be enforced. This was a serious situation to be in.

I was woken up and taken to the glass office, which provided the staff with visibility of the entire day room, entrance and corridors. It was with considerable planning and observation that I had managed to get past this unnoticed two days earlier when I had sneaked to the toilets to cut my wrist. With some surprise, I saw the familiar face of Dr Marks sitting at the desk inside. I tried to focus my eyes and my thoughts, fighting the drugs, in order to answer his questions, but I felt confused and humiliated. I was not allowed to wear my clothes and wore only a nightie, while everyone else was dressed normally, including the other patients. It would be obvious that I had gained weight through the force feeding regimes, and this caused me considerable embarrassment.

One of the Charge-Nurses, Nigel, was trying to paint as black a picture as possible to Dr Marks. He was showing him my blood test results from the paracetamol overdose, and with some animation was saying, "Just look at this! Look at her liver function results! She should have died from this!" As I sat there listening, I remembered another doctor at the Royal Surrey telling me that a person could die up to a fortnight after the overdose and I had not believed him. It was one thing to die when I planned it, but to die some time later when I was not expecting it was entirely different. Dr Marks smiled at me whilst waving Nigel to a seat at the back of the office, making it perfectly clear to him that he wanted to talk to me alone.

"How have you been feeling since I last saw you?" he asked.

"No different," I replied.

I wanted to tell him that life was sheer hell in East House; of how Nigel and another male Charge Nurse had threatened to lock me up, get me drunk and rape me in one of the cells upstairs while everyone else was downstairs. I wanted to tell him about the numerous occasions when other patients had attacked me and how frightened I was. I wanted to tell him that they drugged me to the point that I couldn't walk, could barely move in fact, and regularly had to face the indignity of being undressed by two nurses and locked in an empty cell. I wanted to tell him of the times when I had cried out from within the confines of that cell for help, for comfort, for anything, but nobody came. That if they did come, it was to laugh at me through the two-way mirror in the locked door, or to tell me to shut up, or to come bursting in, manhandling me down and restraining me whilst administering yet another injection. I wanted to tell him that I was surrounded by severely disturbed psychopathic patients, that I was usually the only female on the ward, the only one forced to stay in nightwear - and that it was sending me completely mad. In fact, there were no words which could describe the way I was feeling since I had last seen him.

Sitting there, feeling broken and totally alone, I listened while Dr Marks explained to me that he considered me to be an extremely high-risk patient at the moment and for that reason he was going to agree with Dr Lawton and sign the consent forms for a further Section. Still smiling, he said goodbye to me and I was shown out of the office. Two social workers arrived soon afterwards and, after speaking to me briefly, told me that they also agreed with the sectioning and would be signing their part of the papers accordingly. This was followed by a visit from two people representing the hospital management who came to read me my rights and to tell me that I would be detained at East House for six months on a Section 3.

So, I faced six more months of hell, and then what? Would I ever be able to return to society? I doubted it. I could not imagine finding freedom after this. If I ever did get out, I would return to starvation and die. If I got the opportunity, I would attempt to speed up the process. Death would be the only way of attaining freedom, as ever.

After this I more or less gave up the fight. My medication was increased to the point at which I had neither the strength nor the will power to fight against it. Some days I ate, some I did not. Nobody cared. This was not a unit for treating anorexia, despite the pretence. It was a secure unit; a prison for the mentally insane. It did not even employ normal nurses. The nurses here were predominantly male, on the large side and used to manhandling patients onto the floor and carrying them into cells to be restrained and injected. Treatment consisted of drugs, violent outbursts, followed by more drugs.

And so life went on in East House. During the day I attempted to keep out of the way of the other patients as much as possible by sleeping in a chair facing the wall. Night after night I suffered horrific nightmares which seemed more real to me than my life in East House. I was tormented by the feeling that an evil force seemed to be sucking me towards it. I dreamt that the devil himself told me that he was in control of my life, that I was possessed, and that he had my family in his grip too. I longed to discuss my past and my fears with Dr Lawton but knew that if I did, I would never get out of East House.

Despite the size of the building, there were usually no more than seven patients at a time. They were severely disturbed and unable to be cared for within normal psychiatric units. Some were transferred for a day or two as a punishment for something they had done on another ward, or in another hospital, and the shock of East House was usually enough to encourage co-operation when they were allowed to return. In the early days the same had happened to me, until the staff had simply given up and decided not to bother sending me back.

It was there that I met Lisa, a girl who was about my age (twenty-two), who had been there for several years. When she was admitted she had been very slim and pretty but by the time I knew her, appeared to have no idea of what was going on around her, of who she was, or what she looked like. She wore several layers of clothes, mostly inside out and back to front. Her hair was never brushed, was cut unevenly and stuck up all over her head. She tried to apply make-up to her face, but would smear lipstick across her cheeks and her eyes were black smudges. Without warning, she would run from one side of the room to the other, screaming obscenities and attacking anyone in her path. Despite the similarity of age and gender, Lisa and I had nothing else in common and I never spoke to her during my time at East House. I was terrified of her, as indeed were most of the male patients. Sometimes the unit would allow Lisa to go out for a walk only to receive a frantic phone call saying that she had molested a man in the nearby village, and would somebody come and get her. My greatest fear was that if they made me stay, I would end up like Lisa.

Then there was Ed. Ed looked to be in his 60's and had been living as a tramp before coming to East House. He had no clothes or belongings and so had to wear a pair of dingy grey hospital pyjamas. It soon became apparent that he was more accustomed to being without clothes because he seemed unable to keep them on. He would roll around on the floor moaning and groaning and then charge, quite suddenly, from one end of the room to the other, yelling, as Lisa did. He was a very tall, completely bald man, with sore looking skin that constantly oozed blood. He too seemed unaware of either his surroundings or other people and would even relieve himself in the plant pots in the day room. He was another whom I tried to avoid at all cost.

Much of the time I kept my eyes shut, being completely preoccupied with the thoughts churning inside my head. Sometimes I would watch what was going on around me for fear of getting caught up in it, but usually the others sat in a different room to the one I chose because there they could smoke. They also had a television in the other room, housed in an enormous cabinet with a perspex front to it. Although essential to protect it from the frequent violent outbursts, the panel made it impossible to see the television screen properly but since the audience were so heavily sedated it probably made little difference.   And so the television remained switched on for the majority of the time, pointlessly beaming out through the thick smog of the smoking room.

One morning I was summoned by my consultant Dr Lawton to meet with him and one of his colleagues.   The discussion went from bad to worse.   Dr Lawton asked several questions about events leading up to my admission while the other doctor took notes, and then he began to get very angry with me. "You are behaving like a spoilt 5-year-old!   You refused to cooperate with the treatment on Red Ward earlier this year, and now you are doing exactly the same thing at East House!" This made me livid and I began to shout back at him.   Again he asked me, "Why did you take the overdose?"   I replied, "Because I am sick and tired of being the way I am!   Sick of all the laxatives; sick of my obsession with my weight and food."   In exasperation he said, "It is all within your power to stop, but you are just too bloody minded.   I'm as sick of it as you are!"

"I *know* you are!" I screamed back at him.

Dr Lawton's notes read:

> 'Attitude remains essentially unchanged – attention seeking, self pitying and in essence demanding a magical situation where is eating and not eating at

the same time. Still talks of being possessed by and controlled by her 'obsession' and protests that she cannot help herself.'

I just did not seem to be able to get through to any of them. I was completely frustrated by their inability to comprehend what I was going through. Everyone, including the doctors, assumed that I could simply snap out of the anorexia back to normality, but it was impossible. The more they tried to force me to eat, the more I rebelled — not to be difficult, but because they were not dealing with the underlying issues and I was not able to eat while they remained. (Not that I knew what they were, because as long as I remained anorectic my problems were concealed beneath and I had lost touch with them.) The more the doctors and nurses got cross and fed up, the more hopeless I felt.

"I don't know why I feel like this. I wish you would do something to stop these thoughts. My mind is totally preoccupied with these obsessions and the overwhelming urge for self-destruction that I can't stand anymore of it." The tone of Dr Lawton's voice softened, "If you don't start eating again, you're going to die."

"That's the general idea!" I screamed.

Despite everything I said, they still persisted in punishing me in an attempt to force me to eat. But the more they humiliated me the more they fed my sense of worthlessness and self-disgust, and the more suicidal I felt. I was unable to eat while I felt so low and there was only so much punishment they could hand out before it became meaningless.

Periodically they transferred me out of the secure unit to an acute ward, from where mum would get permission to take me out for an hour or two, but she would always take me somewhere to get something to eat! I would eat a huge amount and then excuse myself while I went to be sick before leaving the restaurant. Somehow I would manage to lose mum and buy a packet of laxatives and in my desperate desire to get rid of the food, I would dash into a public toilet and swallow the entire contents of the packet, washing the pills down with a can of diet coke.

One such day, following the meal and having been sick, I swallowed 60 laxatives before mum took me back to the ward again. I made the mistake of trusting one of the male nurses who had been making attempts to befriend me and decided to tell him how awful I felt at having lost control earlier in the day. To my dismay he responded by saying, "I am really shocked and disappointed by this Beverley, and you know full well that I will have to report this behaviour immediately." I went to bed feeling bitterly let down, although I did not expect much to happen as a consequence of it, so I was rather surprised when I saw the Sister and Dr Rushworth marching towards my bed. It was hard to imagine Dr Rushworth was a real doctor. He was very scruffy and his long black hair and bushy beard made him a very daunting figure. He seemed to revel in my misfortune and genuinely seemed to enjoy punishing me. My heart sank when I saw him approaching.

"Right then Beverley," he said, "I am sending you back to East House for two days to teach you a lesson. You will leave your clothes here on Barker, along with the rest of your belongings." He grinned at me as I looked at him in sheer disbelief, but I was too frightened to argue.

It was very late and pitch black outside when two female nurses arrived from one of the other wards to act as escorts. A male nurse drove the four of us in the pouring rain to East

House.   While we waited for the numerous doors to be unlocked, I got absolutely soaking wet standing there in just my nightie. As soon as I was handed over to the night staff I was led away and locked into a cell on my own. In a state of shock and disbelief, I lay down on the familiar red plastic mattress and looked around at the familiar whitewashed walls. Feelings of utter despair and hopelessness filled the room. I did not care what they did to me anymore, I told myself, because it surely could not get any worse than this. I was in hell itself, and nothing was going to motivate me to eat and get better, nothing.

Doctor Rushworth's notes read:

> '30 May 1987: Beverley reported that she had taken 60 laxatives whilst out with mother today. Medical Registrar RSCH contacted by phone – advise no treatment except observe. However to transfer to EH.   NOT to leave the unit even escorted til reviewed on Monday.
> Carry on with same treatment.'

> '31 May 1987: (am) - Beverley's on hunger strike and refusing to eat. Therefore only allow basic rights for living under Mental Health Act i.e. make-up is a luxury and must be earned by eating and not vomiting.
> 1:1 nursing for 1 hour after meals even in the toilets – patient should be asked to empty bladder before eating.
> Patient is allowed to use toilet privately but meal eating privately is discounted.'

(pm) - Patient says she has a right to her make-up but whilst she is on hunger strike it is imperative we have an accurate assessment of skin colour etc for her well being.'

31 May 1987: Interview with Beverley's mother.
Mother very upset.   I explained the need for someone outside of Beverley to gain control over Beverley.   Beverley's mother was also upset at the thought of no make-up for Beverley but it was eventually explained about her only gain being to be able to hide behind the make-up.

She (Beverley) was described by myself to the mother as using her body and starvation and overdoses to control everyone.

I also explained that once we had control we would also start teaching Beverley some social skills so she would have more appropriate ways of interacting with people.

Beverley's mother was crying when she left but still agrees to support us in insisting on Beverley eating. Programme:

1.   no make-up
2.   make-up returned after 2 meals
3.   Meals to be eaten under 1:1 supervision
4.   1:1 supervision totally for 1 hour after each meal.'

'Monday 1 June 1987: *Today was without make-up and was really awful.   I curled up in my old chair and kept my* *head down. I neither ate nor drank anything. Dr Alikhan came to see me and told me that unless I start eating I will be tube-fed. Charge-nurse Nigel asked me what the point was in being here if I was going to die anyway. I was so uptight that I just shouted at them whenever they approached me. Horrible as this is, I don't want to go home because I so desperately want to be free of this obsession and I know that's not possible at home. I don't know what to do because I am desperate to lose more weight, but I don't want to return to bingeing and vomiting either if I am discharged...'*

Dr Alikhan's notes read:

> '1 June 1987: Seen.
> Has not eaten anything today, is very angry about taking her make-up away. Wants to remain in hospital but refusing to eat or cooperate with the treatment programme. To discuss with Dr Lawton.'

Nursing Record reads:

> '30 May 1987: (am) - Well behaved this am. Had a long chat with nursing staff. 1:1 obs maintained. No diet taken.
>
> (pm) - Went out with mother. No diet taken - says she ate whilst out with mother.
>
> (Nocte) - confessed to taking 60 laxatives while out with mother. Dr Rushworth contacted and saw Beverley. To be transferred to EH until further notice.

31 May 1987: - Seen at length by Dr Rushworth and mother. In order to make some progress Beverley was told that her make-up will be withdrawn from her until she eats 2 full meals and has kept them down. Beverley appeared angry and swore at Dr Rushworth. Her sister, Louisa shouted at staff over the withdrawal of her make-up. Mother reluctant to agree but eventually did. Dr Lawton has been informed and agreed. Will see Beverley tomorrow.

1 June 1987: (am) - Has made no effort to eat despite removal of her make up. Sat in chair all morning quiet and withdrawn.

(pm) - Seen by Dr Alikhan re her persistent refusal to eat. She was completely unresponsive, only saying she would not eat until she got her make-up back. It was explained that she would only get it back if she ate. She reluctantly agreed to try to eat on the condition that she was treated for her 'inner feelings' afterwards. It was stressed that she could approach nursing staff for counselling at any time and that once she was eating we could better assess her physical and mental state. She agreed to this but when her meal arrived she wrapped it up and was found trying to throw it in the bin. She was then given a jam sandwich of which she ate very little and then also disposed of the rest of this in the bin

A few days later:

… '*I decided to try and eat to see if that would encourage them to help me, but when I did they were delighted, telling me that I would soon be well enough to go home! They have no idea. Nothing has changed. They still think the problem is the eating.*'

Then:

… '*I was trying to maintain control of my eating and my feelings, but I lost it and started to eat toast at breakfast. I felt so terrified that I just wanted to die. I cannot bear the sensation of losing control. I do not know which is worse — to get discharged before it goes any further and go back to living the way I was before, or to stick this out, not knowing if they are ever going to help me or whether I will just end up fat and still feel the same.*'

'*What do they think they are doing to me? Why can't they understand? I am so desperately frightened and unhappy. I tried to cooperate and eat but when I couldn't cope with it, nobody tried to help me. I cannot bear being like this. I am not doing it on purpose to irritate them. I just want them to try and understand and help me. This is not helping at all — it makes me feel worse.*'

It was at that point that I decided to start keeping back my medication under my tongue to save up enough to kill myself.

'**Tuesday 9 June 1987**: *I am sick of it, all of it. I hate them all, they are making my life hell and I have had enough.*

Now they have even taken away the little they let me have yesterday. I will not eat or drink again! They are reducing me to nothing and that's just how I feel; everyone can see just how worthless I am. I told them that this is not going to work; whatever they do to me, it won't work. My life was hell before I came in here and now they're making it worse. If any of them try to talk me round, I tell them that to eat means accepting life and I DO NOT. I reject life because I am not worthy of it. I told them that I have to destroy myself, although I don't know why. When I eat, I feel like I am losing control and the obsession and craving for food becomes totally unbearable. I have to binge and vomit to punish myself for it — punish myself for accepting life into my body, where there is none.'

I managed to keep some make-up hidden in a shoe under the bed just in case it was taken away again, and each day I put on the tiniest amount. One day it was spotted by the Charge Nurse, who demanded to know where I had got it from and told me to go and wash it off. I was so cross that I fled out of the room grabbing some clothes off a chair and the tablets that I'd been saving, and took a flying jump straight out of a ground floor window. I ran to some bushes, where I quickly pulled the clothes on over the top of the nightie I was wearing. A nurse started in hot pursuit after me, shouting at one of the gardeners to help her catch me. I had no time to do up the skirt and just held on to it as I ran, trying to keep it from tripping me up. As it became clear that I had managed to out run them, the nurse shouted after me that she was going back to call the police.

Once I was alone, I didn't know what to do or where to go. I hadn't managed to save up many pills by then but I took all the ones I had and the effect came very quickly. My legs felt like dead weights and I could barely keep my eyes open. I was collected and there were no kind words, they just went berserk. They threw all my belongings into bin bags, shoved me into a car and drove me straight to East House and dumped me there. I was taken away, locked up in a cell and left to recover from the effects of the drugs. I felt confused and lonely, crying for hours on end. With each passing moment I was falling apart a little bit further. I was dying slowly from the inside out. It felt as though there was nothing left of me but an empty shell.

'They are all torturing me. They all hate me. As soon as I get out of here I will kill myself. I'm already dying inside. I'm forcing in food, forcing in life where there is no life, no room for life. I feel like I am not really here and do not even exist.'

Nursing Record reads:

> 7 June 1987: Says she feels she can't get better. Hasn't taken any visible diet today.

> 8 June 1987: (am) - No diet taken.

> (pm) - It was explained that because she has taken no diet that her visits from relatives and friends are being restricted.

> 9 June 1987: No diet taken. Says that she doesn't feel that the programme will help her. Her programme was discussed and the next step of

privileges was explained. Beverley said that she doesn't feel ready to start eating because of the feelings of guilt she has. Said she's afraid of fellow patient.

10 June 1987: (am) - At 8.30am Beverley was asked to get dressed into her day clothes in preparation for attending Occupational Therapy. Nursing staff observing pt but got called away - Beverley decided to quickly grab some clothes from her locker and escaped out of the window and changed into her clothes in the fields and quickly disappeared. Missing person procedure carried out. Later at 11.10am Dr Alikhan phoned to say Beverley was in her waiting room and was refusing to return. She has been complaining of the treatment and her programme and that removing her make-up from her is not going to make her eat. Eventually returned to ward with nurse escort. Was asked to go back into night clothes.
Dr Alikhan contacted for further management as pt had taken OD of meds. To be nursed in EH.'

Back in East House, things were quiet with few patients in and practically one-to-one nursing care. There were two staff teams each managed by two Charge Nurses at a time. One of those teams was managed by Nigel and Shane, a double act of unpredictable nature. Sometimes they deliberately caused trouble to make a patient react negatively, resulting in such a fuss that they could justify stepping in to restrain and drug the patient concerned. They were rude and condescending. I think they assumed that none of the patients on such a ward would know what they were up to because we were either so disturbed or drugged up to the eyeballs, but I knew exactly what they were doing. I felt very vulnerable as the only female on the ward most of the time and they knew it. The pair of them continuously flirted and were rudely suggestive in front of me. At times it was hard to know if they were joking or whether they meant it. There was no-one to turn to for help and nobody would believe a patient on East House anyway if I said anything.

Dr Lawton, Dr Alikhan and two of the charge-nurses interviewed me one morning at great length, telling me that my Section would expire the following day. They wanted me to remain in East House as an informal patient. They said that I could have a certain amount of freedom restored to me, like going for a walk sometimes, but that the programme would remain unchanged. This bothered me. It was not fair to be an informal patient on a secure ward and I felt frustrated and angry. They knew that they could keep me on East House without a Section because there were no beds available elsewhere and I had nowhere to live if I left. I was still acutely depressed and as I lay awake that night, feeling confused and desperate, I knew what I was going to do.

After breakfast the following morning, I asked to be allowed out for a walk. They let me go so I walked straight to the chemist and bought two packets of paracetamol and a bottle of orange juice. I sat in a football field where I swallowed the forty-eight pills. I stayed in the field for a couple of hours before beginning to feel very ill. I then decided to walk back to the ward and hoped that they would not realise anything was wrong. Feeling progressively worse as the day wore on, I remained curled up in my usual chair, saying nothing to anyone.

Finally Nigel glanced at me as he walked across the room before rushing over. Bending down to me, he asked, "Right, what have you taken and how many?" By this time I was feeling so ill that I actually thought it would be too late for them to do anything. I smiled up at him as I told him. His face fell and for a split second he did not believe me. As soon as he realised that I was not joking, a sense of urgency set in. As he rushed to the office to call for an ambulance, he shouted to the others, alerting them of the situation and calling for help. Everyone seemed to go into a panic, rushing around, and it began to feel like a dream that I was not really part of. I tried to protest about being put in the ambulance, but I was feeling so ill that I didn't care what they did to me. One of the male nurses was asked to escort me to the hospital. Bob was an enormous heavyweight, whom I had never spoken to and now was not the time to get to know each other. He looked acutely embarrassed about being with me, so I tried to shut out the fact that he was there by keeping my eyes shut.

The moment we arrived in the casualty unit I was wheeled into a treatment room and they wasted no time in performing a stomach wash-out. All the time Bob stayed by my side, as he had been instructed, although he never said a word to me. If they thought I still had it in me to run, they were very much mistaken. Bob waited until he had the results of the blood tests to phone through to East House. Eventually a doctor came to see me to explain the serious implications of the results and, in a matter of fact tone, he informed me that my chances of survival were minimal. They would put up a drip to counteract the effects of the paracetamol on my liver but it may already be too late to save me. I tried hard not to show any emotion on my face, but in reality I was very scared.

Bob's expression never changed once until the relief showed when they told him that I would be admitted and that he could go back to East House.

The whole incident passed like a surreal nightmare. I already felt dead. It seemed as if nobody in the world cared if I lived or died, and the thoughts that had plagued my mind before the suicide attempt remained as black and tormenting as ever. There was not a waking moment of peace within me, as there were no moments of peace within the walls of East House. It felt as if the building itself screamed out with anguish and pain from the many tortured souls that had inhabited its rooms.

Two days after my return to East House from the general hospital, I could stand it no longer. I fled from the dayroom, escaping the eyes of the nurses in the glass office, slamming shut the cubicle door of the dingy toilet. In a state of wild frenzy I began to cut...

Chapter 10

Discharged

I **SAW PATIENTS COME AND GO** at East House and as Ed, the tramp, was discharged, rational and smartly dressed, I posed the question to Charge-Nurse Nigel, "How come they are all getting better and I just stay the same?" Nigel shrugged wearily, "I was thinking the same thing actually."

Some two and half months since my admission to East House, Dr Lawton asked another consultant to come and see me on the ward for a second opinion. "You've been here some time, Beverley, can you describe to me how you are feeling now?" Dr Anderson asked. And so I told him, "I want to erase myself. I hate myself and must destroy myself. I feel like a big black cloud is coming down over me and suffocating me like a blanket. I feel like I've been kicked in the stomach and all the breath has been knocked out of me. I'm going to rot away in here, I can't cope and have resigned myself to it, to hopelessness."

"It is quite apparent," he replied, "that nothing has changed at all, which is exactly what Dr Lawton has told me and why he has asked me to come and see you. You see, it leads us to the conclusion that this is not a psychiatric problem. We are not prepared to see you waste anymore of your life in here because you are becoming institutionalised, which will be no good for you in the long term. Therefore my recommendation to Dr Lawton is going to be that we discharge you today. I want you to have a think for half an hour about where you could go, then you are to leave the unit to make some phone calls on your own."

"But I don't have anywhere to go!" I cried, totally shocked by his announcement. "I'm now divorced and I haven't got a home."

"I think we should at least give her until tomorrow to sort this out," stepped in Nigel. "Okay, fine. Tomorrow. But I am going to be writing in your notes that no matter what you do to yourself in the future, we will not admit you back here at The Grove. You will not be able to manipulate the situation by harming yourself in order to force us to change our minds because it is time to stand up and fight this for yourself. Whatever you do when you leave here, you will be accountable for. We are not going to be responsible for your death, do you understand?"

Dr Anderson's notes read:

> '20 July 1987: I saw this unfortunate rather immature girl today at the request of Dr Lawton. In my view she has a very damaged personality and has a great deal of insight. However she is confused about various conflicts and has an intense need to control her life. I am sure her upbringing and parent's relationship, or lack of it, is at the root of her problem. She has learnt to 'remain ill' to seek help continuously.

I feel that as long as the health service is prepared to allow her to be ill she will be. In her best interest, a decision is to be taken not to admit her. This will give her a chance to think of other options of coping.'

I really couldn't believe what I was hearing. Ridiculous as it sounded, I didn't know how I was going to survive! It threw me into a terrible panic and I felt that there had been a huge miscarriage of justice. Following Dr Anderson's report, Dr Lawton came to see me before I left East House for good. "I have to say, Beverley, that I agree wholeheartedly with Dr Anderson. You have got no better in all the time you have been here and all we are doing is keeping you alive, which isn't what the NHS is for! There is nothing else we can do for you, so I think this is for the best."

I was not going to be offered any further support even on an out-patient basis. Generally the nurses had been as surprised at the decision as I had been, openly expressing their concern and disapproval. My mum was devastated by the decision but agreed to take me home and I left angry, confused and very frightened, but intent on one thing - to go back into starvation and to lose as much weight as possible.

It may have seemed a strange decision to have made at the time but clearly methods at The Grove had not helped the situation, having in fact made it very much worse. It emphasised the fact that nothing and nobody could do it for me. But I couldn't do it for me either.

Chapter 11

The Miracle

Two evenings after my return from East House my mother received a surprise phone call from an old school friend with whom I had lost contact several years earlier. Coming across my mother's telephone number, Marie had nervously decided to ring to find out literally if I was still alive. We didn't meet immediately because I always hid away following discharge from hospital until I'd lost sufficient weight to feel I was 'me' again. In the meantime I had contacted Rob, the heroin addict that I had met on Red Ward the previous year. Rob was struggling to come clean, which I knew but selfishly didn't care about because I rang him up asking him to supply me with drugs. The temptation was too great for him and he agreed to meet me.

I told Danny that I wanted the house for a couple of days which he agreed to, and Rob took me to the home of a dealer he knew to buy a gram of speed. Within the grubby interior of his flat, the slovenly dealer wanted us to use it there and then with him but, probably sensing my fear and the need to protect me, Rob admirably managed to persuade him to just give us the packet.

Back at the house I watched Rob meticulously, almost lovingly, preparing the speed for injecting, with utmost fascination. Unable to wait a moment longer, Rob injected himself first before dropping the syringe into a mug of boiling water that he had already prepared. As he tied a tourniquet around my arm, I felt incredibly nervous. I watched as he began to inject the cloudy fluid into my vein. I could actually feel the drug travelling up my arm before exploding upon impact upon my brain, like some parasitic entity let loose into my bloodstream.

"Wow, this is better than sex!" I exclaimed, wickedly. Rob smiled. Poor chap knew only too well what that first hit was like; knowing also what would follow too. Hour upon hour went by as I sat pinned to the chair watching the weird and terrifying images before my eyes. "Just let yourself go, Bev. Relax!" Rob mumbled as he watched me, vaguely amused for a few brief moments as I struggled with what I was seeing, before he too slipped back into his own delusionary world.

Despite the fact that I found it a pretty unpleasant experience once I'd moved beyond the initial hit, I was hell-bent on self-destruction and whilst on speed my mind was too preoccupied to think about bingeing. Hence I had found another useful ploy to aid me in my quest to lose weight, regardless of the consequences it might have on my body.

I had left East House on a considerable amount of medication and when I wasn't able to get hold of any speed, I crushed up my Valium tablets, mixed them with a little tap water from the bathroom, and injected the coarse powder straight into my veins. This caused the most excruciating headaches I have ever experienced, or would ever want to. On one such occasion having just injected myself, I was completely unable to get up off the floor for the pain, cradling my head in my hands and moaning.

♣

Marie suggested that we ought to go to her church as they would be able to help me but I wasn't at all convinced. I didn't believe for one minute that any church could possibly help, but I was willing to accompany Marie if it made her happy, and I was desperate.

Once the service drew to a close, Marie pushed her way to the front to seek the advice of the minister. Feeling very uncomfortable about this, I tried to look inconspicuous and keep my distance but the minister wanted to introduce me to one of the elders' wives, Ann. Ann suggested that Marie and I came to her house two days later for a chat, which I agreed to more out of embarrassment than anything.

Ann had arranged for another lady to be there as well. I had no preconceived ideas about the meeting having, in all honesty, not given it much thought since Sunday. It had been my 23rd birthday on the Monday and Marie had organised a surprise party for me at her flat so I'd completely forgotten about it. So when they simply ushered me into the sitting room and asked me to sit down whilst they stood around me to pray, I felt acutely uncomfortable and expectant of nothing. The three women, Marie included, prayed in tongues for forty-five minutes or so. Meanwhile I felt nothing, looked around the room and didn't pray for anything myself — I could have been anywhere other than where I was right then for my own lack of feeling about what was going on.

Their prayer came to an unexpected pause as Ann posed a question, "Would you like to ask Jesus into your life, Beverley?" Believing that this was something that I had already done as a teenager, and seeing no harm in repeating it if it made them all happy, I said that I would. Ann led me in a very short and simple prayer. Then came the crunch-line: "Will you say sorry to God for all the sin in your life?" Intense anger rose in me as the thought flashed through my mind: none of this is my fault - all of my problems are from the consequences of other people's sins! Instead of arguing though, and to my astonishment, I found myself nodding rather meekly in contrast to the thought I'd just had. Ann led me in another prayer, very non-specific, but gently encompassing all sin in a simple prayer of repentance, much to my relief.

The moment the words were spoken, a remarkable and quite inexplicable event occurred. Although I had not been conscious of it prior to the prayer, I became aware of what seemed to be a heavy blackness surrounding me as it began to lift. It was as if I had been sitting there underneath a blanket and somebody had just got hold of one corner and flipped it right off my head. I had gotten so used to that blanket that I wasn't always aware of its presence until I felt what it was like to be without it. And it suddenly felt as if the sun was shining! I must have been subconsciously aware of it, as I had told Dr Anderson before leaving East House: "I feel like a big black cloud is coming down over me and suffocating me like a blanket."

Something spiritually significant and very exciting had just taken place — I had been healed!

♣

Whilst I knew in my heart that I had been healed that day, to an outsider the struggles recorded in my diary over the weeks and months to come conflicted in every possible way with a healing having ever taken place. What had changed was that I had gained the will to live and this was such a turn-around in thinking that was hugely momentous and awesome at the time.

Certainly I became desperately frustrated with the way my life had become and wanted an instantaneous change. But there was to be no sudden change in actual behaviour, or to my physical state of health because I remained starving and addicted to laxatives and tranquillizers. There were still times when I felt extremely ill, but in contrast to before when I had gone to bed praying to die, I would head to the church where I prayed for further healing with Ann and her husband, Ken.

I didn't want to die anymore and that was the first step to turning my life around.

Chapter 12

A Life Repossessed

ANN AND KEN arranged for me to move into the home of a young Christian family from the church so that I had constant prayer support around the clock. Ken made it quite clear that there were house rules for me to abide by, namely: getting up by 8 a.m., being in by 11 p.m., attendance at both Sunday morning and evening services, the Saturday morning service at 7.30 a.m., mid-week evening house-group as well as the mid-week lunchtime service, and there was to be no smoking in the house! There were no rules about eating, except that I was to sit at the table with the family when they had meals, whether I chose to eat or not. All of this was very hard to accept because I had lived mostly away from home since the age of seventeen and it was particularly difficult to allow anyone else to have any control over my life after my time spent in East House.

Melita and her family were warm and friendly towards me. The children were cheerful and noisy and seemed to be excited about the prospect of me coming to live with them. I had no experience of children whatsoever, and instead of appreciating what they were taking on by agreeing to accept me into their family, wondered instead how I was going to cope with them, rather selfishly. I settled in quickly though, growing very fond of Melita. Initially I refused to eat anything but gradually, as we prayed together and talked through issues, I began to eat small amounts with her. I was convinced however that everybody would be able to see that I was growing fatter by the day and it caused enormous anxiety for me.

I met weekly with Ann to discuss any problems that had arisen over the course of the previous week, whilst she made notes and tried to look for familiar patterns and triggers. Every week I complained about the 11 p.m. curfew, and every week I was told that it would remain unchanged! Ann and Ken had worked in a Christian rehabilitation home for people with addictions and had plenty of experience with anorexia. Whilst they knew the importance of having firm boundaries in place, I felt like an adult being treated like a naughty child that kept disobeying the rules. If I got back late, I wouldn't go in at all for fear of being reprimanded and would make the matter worse by sleeping outside in my car all night.

Obviously they were concerned about the negative spiritual influences I came under every time I went home, which was undoubtedly destructive, and so Ann and Ken advised against home visits in the short term. Melita spent hours talking and praying with me, which I often repaid with ingratitude and selfishness when the going got tough. Not only did I suffer with paranormal interference, which I had grown accustomed to, but there was the danger that I would inadvertently bring it to bear on the rest of the family.

Fairly early on in my rehabilitation, mum telephoned me at Melita's to tell me that she had heard in the news about a girl who had died of organ failure as a consequence of taking laxatives. I became extremely distressed and angry that I hadn't died from laxative abuse, and despite the fact that I had gained the will to live, made the astonishing decision to hand my life back to Satan. I became uncommunicative and curled up in a chair, feeling as if my soul had been thrown to the wind and I was nothing more than a zombie. In fact it felt pretty much as it had done back at East House. As the memories flooded back, I told God that the battle was too difficult, that He and the devil would have to fight it out between themselves, I didn't care which one of them won as long as it was 100% either way. I became so confused that Melita rang Ann and Ken for help, who came straight over to pray for me.

I hadn't realised that God had already won the battle and that He had already done all that was necessary for me to be free. It certainly didn't feel like it right then and Satan didn't want me knowing this truth. My feelings and mood swings would soar from joy to utter hopelessness and despair, with suicidal thoughts continuing to tempt me. This was not surprising coming from the occult background I had and the fact that Satan didn't want to let go of me. I became so frustrated with my own desperate need for help and my inability to cope with the intensity of the mood swings, I determined to find the tranquillizers that Melita had confiscated and hidden from me. When she left me briefly in the house alone, it suddenly dawned on me where she had hidden them and within minutes of locating them, I had swallowed 30 Valium tablets. By the time Melita returned, I was barely able to stand up straight.

On the advice of Howard, a Consultant Surgeon at the church, Ann and Ken took me back to their own house and left me to sleep off the effects on their settee. Despite the fact that we all knew a healing had taken place, the onslaught of attacks were draining for everyone and Ann and

Ken arranged for me to stay with Howard and Elizabeth to give Melita's family a break, as well as to give me a change of scenery after the OD. While Howard was at work at the hospital, Elizabeth was at home bringing up their boys and was able to spend time with me while they were at school.

One of the elders in the church was a GP and he took over my medical care. Maurice met with me on a weekly basis at the surgery to see how I was doing and tried to teach me how to depend on God as opposed to medication. This was particularly useful coming from a doctor because I felt he was able to differentiate between what was psychological and what was spiritual, and he was convinced that it was all mostly the latter. One of the first things Maurice decided to do was to take me off Valium because he thought that it was too big a risk while I felt the way I did. Acknowledging the fact that he was being very hard on me by not allowing me to withdraw gradually, Maurice explained that it was for the best. He wasn't particularly surprised about the OD, telling me that he had expected it and warned me of the likelihood of there being many more downfalls yet in the recovery process.

For the time being, I went back into starvation because at least my emotions were slightly less chaotic than when I was eating. There were to be so many tears shed between us, but so much love given from Melita, Ann and Ken, Howard and Elizabeth, and so many others who got drawn in to helping me. If they grew tired, cross or frustrated with the intensity of the level of support I needed, it never showed. I was confident that what God had begun in me would be completed and that in all things God worked for the good of those who love him. (Phil.1:6, Rom.8:28) I clung precariously to these words at times but they were my lifeline.

When I look back at my behaviour, the terrible frustration, depression and selfishness, it makes me feel very guilty. I'm glad that I was not aware of just how long it was going to take to recover, or just how hard the battle was going to be, because I probably would have given up had I known! But I had hope, and I knew God wasn't going to leave a job half-done.

Whilst Maurice and others were spending a great deal of time teaching me more about God, I often found that I wasn't able to retain what they said, as well as misinterpreting what they told me. Howard also thought that I needed to get a job and to help facilitate this he took me to work with him at the hospital. I worked on a voluntary basis as I gained experience working alongside Howard's own secretary. Howard also offered to perform a skin graft on my arm to cover up the scarring as my arm had become quite distorted in shape by the sheer quantity of scars concentrated over the underside of my left forearm. It looked absolutely dreadful but with the surgery, hope of a more normal future was extended to me again. As Maurice had predicted however, it was not going to be plain sailing. Invariably, slip-ups continued to occur after visits back home.

Saturday 19 March 1988: '*I had a bad day at mum's today. She collected me from Howard and Elizabeth's at lunch-time and took me to a pub. I didn't want her to know that I was still struggling with my food, so had some nuts while she had a meal. Then she bought some chocolate and I ate some of it with her but made myself sick. When we got back to her house I felt really ill in there, my head was spinning and I'm sure I was under attack. Mum knew that I would miss tea with Howard and Elizabeth, so I had to eat some toast to* *keep her happy, but by the time I got back I felt so uptight. I became obsessed with the need to punish myself for the toast. I took an old razor blade to my bedroom and lay on the bed trying to do anything that would take my mind off it, but couldn't. I was going to do it, so I prayed that God would save me.*

I started to cut and felt no pain at all. I was obsessed with the blood. I covered the bedclothes with a towel but I was actually able to stop before it got too deep and ask for help. I called Howard a few times from outside their bedroom door but they were asleep and didn't hear. I didn't know what to do because if I went back to my room, I knew that I would cut deeper. There was a raging violence inside me that was threatening to erupt if I didn't cut further.

I sat on the landing outside their bedroom door, staring at the cut and becoming more obsessed with it. I began pulling it apart, digging my fingers into it and pulling out the tiny globules of fat. My hands and arms were covered in blood, as were my nightie and dressing-gown. My thinking became further distorted as it occurred to me that I was pulling out actual fatty lumps to compensate for the fat I'd gained in the toast earlier.

I snapped to my senses and realised that the situation was getting out of control and screamed for Howard. He came rushing out of the bedroom and nearly had a fit when he saw the blood. He got Elizabeth up and both of them took me downstairs to the kitchen, where Howard insisted that Elizabeth cleaned me up before he could bear to look at me. Howard was rolling about on the floor moaning at the mess of the blood, saying he couldn't bear it because the sight of blood made him sick! Despite the state I was in, this made us all laugh!

Elizabeth cleaned me up while Howard got his equipment ready, gave me a local anaesthetic, and stitched it up. It was in the early hours of the morning by then and he went back to bed while Elizabeth stayed up with me to pray. Howard gave me a big hug in the morning but I felt very depressed about it all and a complete failure.'

Despite my awareness of a healing having taken place, the suicidal feelings were as intense, if not more so, than ever before. Prayer ministry took place on a daily basis, dealing with the thoughts and feelings as they surfaced and each crisis situation as it arose. After each episode of ministry I felt renewed with increased ability to go on, before collapsing into the depths of despair by the following day. I was simply unable to retain any of what they taught me and progress made continuously seemed to slip away. Often during these prayer ministry sessions I felt surges of anger and violence welling up within me and, on one such occasion, I begged them to stop, saying that if they didn't, I would hit one of them. Instead, it felt as if I had been slapped around the face and my body jerked back away into my chair by the impact of it. I heard God say, "No! It's time to move forwards now." I could feel the dark cloak over me again as it was whipped away, leaving me standing outside of it. But I stood naked and vulnerable and all I wanted to do was to run back under the blanket again, to hide and sink back into my illness, where I was used to being. God's voice spoke again: "No more! You've had too many years of illness. It is time to start moving forwards."

Unfortunately the rage within me refused to subside as the prayer recommenced and Ann and Ken, along with their friend from the prayer ministry team, decided to seek the

Lord for deliverance on my behalf. The frenzy within me magnified until, feeling as if I would literally kill one of them unless they stopped, I warned them again against continuing. Insisting that God would protect them, they persisted. My muscles paralysed, my body convulsed and I thought I would vomit. The evil spirit holding onto me tightened its grip around my neck, choking me. I was terrified because I knew something was refusing to give me up. Despite their faith and willingness to persevere, the situation remained unchanged and so instead they prayed for protection for us all until they could continue again another day.

When I awoke the following day, my throat was still sore and I felt traumatised and frightened by the whole experience. Their attempts to perform deliverance ministry seemed to suggest that I was possessed and this was something I couldn't handle. I was trying to come to terms with my occult past without the need to lean on anorexia to cover it up and now I was being forced to face the consequences of the occult activity as well, and I couldn't. The mere suggestion of being possessed made the whole thing feel as if it just wasn't worth it because it was way too big to handle.

My past seemed to create a springboard within my mind for all the teaching to bounce back off, to be lost completely from my memory. All I could think about was the fact that I was yet again surrounded by evil spirits that controlled my life, as they always had done, and there was nothing I could do about it.

But bit-by-bit progress was being made and on Sunday 17 April 1988 I was baptised. Friends that I had only ever kept in touch with through my letter writing came to see me being baptised and to hear me give my testimony.   This event had a dramatic effect because everybody in the church then knew of my healing. So many people wanted to talk to me, hug me, kiss me; so many people with tears in their eyes as they heard of the terrible misery of life within the confines of a secure unit and the miracle God had performed.

This was a lot to live up to in the coming days and within less than a fortnight disaster struck. Howard had gone away with Elizabeth for a few days, leaving me to get on with working in his office alongside his secretary. I was surprised and flattered to be asked out by one of the junior doctors and over the course of the next few days I missed a couple of church meetings, as well as returning home well after the 11 p.m. curfew. Melita was furious, Howard returning to report my misdemeanour to Ken. Presenting the truth of the matter to me, Ken insisted that my behaviour had to change because it wasn't helping me or anybody else. Rightly so, he told me that I was an embarrassment to Howard after the lengths to which he had gone to get me a job at the hospital. I was too fragile to cope with such criticism unfortunately and instead of thinking about what had been said and learning from it, I was consumed instead with the need to run away and hide. I couldn't live up to their expectations, I wasn't good enough, never would be and nobody understood. These more familiar thoughts kicked in and I gave in to them, allowing them to take hold. I went straight to the chemist and bought two packets of Paracetamol, returning to my room at Melita's to swallow them all and go to bed to die.

Melita was still cross with me and so left me to myself for the remainder of the day. Later that evening I began vomiting blood every fifteen minutes. I was white, shaking uncontrollably and as our paths crossed on the landing for the first time that day, Melita's face fell. Her first reaction was to ring Ken, who, assuming it was no different to the last time, reassured Melita that all I needed to do was to sleep it off. "It's too late for that!" I hissed at her angrily. Turning my bedroom upside down, she uncovered the empty bottles of Paracetamol underneath my bed and phoned Maurice. Maurice advised her that there was indeed no time to lose and phoned for the ambulance himself. Paramedics arrived whilst I was still being sick and dragged me off to the local A & E, much to my annoyance and without any cooperation on my part.

Feeling very angry with everyone, and bitterly let down, I refused to allow them to perform a stomach wash-out, telling them it was a waste of time since I had ingested the tablets several hours earlier. The blood levels were dangerously high though and it was explained to me that without the antidote, and even with it, I might haemorrhage and die. As I began to calm down I conceded and allowed them to put up the drip but not to the stomach wash out.

Nobody at the church was told what I had done. I didn't contact my family because I didn't want to disillusion them about my healing. Apart from Melita, who dropped in a few bits and pieces for me a couple of days later, nobody visited. Except, that is, for one man who had been so touched by my testimony that he had made a point of looking out for me every Sunday afterwards to give me a hug. When I didn't turn up that weekend, for some reason he decided to go to the hospital to see if I had been admitted. To my amazement, he sat for a considerable length of time beside my bed playing a guitar and singing worship songs to me, whilst I vomited. It was the most bizarre experience and although I had never felt quite as miserable as I did during those few days, I was touched by his faith and love for me.

Yet again God saved me, spewing me back out onto the path of recovery that I had strayed from temporarily, as Jonah was spewed from the mighty fish when he had also tried to run from the path that had been set for him. Recovery was so hard, harder than being ill. The church refused my membership application a week later, something that again caused me anger, rejection and frustration. Whilst I was doing all that I could to cooperate, at times they didn't seem to understand at all. The rules and boundaries that had been set for my own good were beginning to get me down and annoy me, and served only as a hindrance. Failing to understand why the boundaries had been set, I decided to move out and do it my own way.

I moved in with some non-Christians about my own age and at the same time I was given a new salaried position at the hospital. I was to be the only medical secretary responsible to about thirty anaesthetists and would be based on the opposite side of town to where Howard was. The job appeared to be an answer to prayer, but could I cope with it? I was very nervous and wanted so much to succeed but I really wasn't ready for it. The jump was too big a one for me at that point, on top of which, I had placed myself in a position of total isolation at a time when I needed all the support I could get.

Chapter 13

My Boys

WHAT ON EARTH was I doing working in a hospital surrounded by doctors when I was actually still deeply traumatised by my in-patient experiences, which had resulted in a phobia of doctors? When my accommodation arrangements fell apart, Alison, a friend I'd made at the hospital, let me stay in one of the doctor's on-call flats temporarily. Finding myself hemmed-in twenty-four hours a day, with doctors everywhere I turned, it was impossible to separate the patient from the medical secretary. During the day I found myself too nervous to speak to the doctors that I worked for, then, outside of working hours, I returned to being the patient. I would self-harm before bleeping whoever was on-call from my own department to request help from them.

Probably because they didn't want to offend Howard they tolerated this very difficult situation and tried to support me for a considerable period of time. But my thought life was in turmoil; voices continued to bombard me day in, day out, telling me I must die. Ann and Ken told me to pray harder which seemed to imply lack of faith on my part, but I was praying without letting up. I grew tired of listening to them all telling me to depend more on God. Why didn't they understand? The voices wouldn't shut up and I couldn't cope with it anymore. I loved Jesus with all my heart; in fact I always had done, even as a child, but I had been so deceived.

I was eating regularly (although not huge amounts) and had stopped abusing laxatives and tranquillizers, so huge progress had been made but I was terribly depressed. I felt so ugly and unable to cope with living a normal life, being me, a person who wasn't anorectic. I had lost my identity. Who was I anyway without anorexia? What I was, was terribly lonely. With my family and marriage torn apart and with no home to speak of except the on-call flat, I was spending hour upon hour on my own. Finally, having given up on trying to deal with it spiritually, I registered with a new doctor and told him that I was hearing voices and was completely obsessed with death! Not surprisingly, I was admitted that same evening to a new psychiatric hospital where they had never heard of me.

But how should I behave as a patient now that I wasn't anorectic? How could I convince them of my desperate need to rid myself of the thoughts and what they were driving me to if there were no outward symptoms of illness – as least as I perceived it? What was wrong with me? They clearly didn't see me as psychotic but the church hadn't been able to stop the thoughts either. I was a terrible patient, causing mayhem and self-harming at every opportunity because I thought that they needed to *see* how awful I felt in order to know. It wasn't long before I found myself Sectioned again.

Feeling torn between the security this offered, and the terrible fear of losing control again to another psychiatrist, I rang my mum and insisted that she had the Section annulled and demand my discharge. This she did and I returned once again to my lonely existence in the on-call flat, typing clinic letters during the day for a different set of doctors. I felt like I was going mad, madder in fact than I'd ever felt before as an anorectic.

Occasionally I would turn up at a mid-week church housegroup, but I couldn't concentrate and would generally fall asleep. I wasn't really aware of anybody else in the group so when Paul asked me if I would accompany him to his company dinner, I had no idea who he was. I would not have been able to identify anyone in that group if I met them outside of it. How much of life I was missing due to my disordered thinking and depression alarmed me.

Paul had become a Christian at about the same time as me and had been present when I'd given my testimony and been baptised, so there was nothing to hide from him. He arrived to take me out, and as he opened the car door for me I saw a small gift-wrapped present sitting on the passenger seat for me. I wasn't used to being treated like this and several more dates were to follow. He didn't discuss my past, nor did he comment on my weight, my make-up or my clothes; he didn't try to take advantage of me, treating me with respect and like a friend. In Paul, I was to find a companion for life who could be totally and completely trusted, no matter what I threw at him.

We went out to eat several times a week and whilst my weight increased rapidly, causing me considerable distress, I continued to eat normally, beginning to actually enjoy food I hadn't eaten in years. Paul never seemed to notice, or probably more to the point, didn't say a word about my weight as it went up, making it safe for me to let my body adjust. We became pretty much inseparable outside of working hours; if we didn't go out to eat, or to the cinema, then we would spend the evenings in my on-call room watching the television, until I had to force him to go home.

Despite this new friendship however, I remained severely depressed and was admitted back to the hospital yet again for further treatment. I had gained three and a half stone since my last admission and a rather cocky junior psychiatrist, who obviously recognised me, arrived to go through the usual admission procedure. "What have you done to yourself?" he exclaimed as he looked at me — with disgust, it seemed to me. Paul looked at me hesitantly as I blushed. So I must be fat! The thought hit me like a brick out of nowhere because I had tried so hard to ignore it and I really had no idea what I looked like. The thought that I was disgusting after all overwhelmed me and self-loathing hit hard.

This time they performed electro-convulsive therapy, ECT. Treatment occurred twice weekly when an anaesthetist from my own department at the general hospital would arrive to assist, much to my enormous embarrassment. On the morning of the treatment patients from various wards around the hospital would be rounded up in a minibus and driven to a newer building where the ECT machine was kept. This was a new dimension of degradation and humiliation. Half a dozen or so patients would be taken to a room and left to wait their turn. I was the only young person being given this treatment at the time and I would sit there looking around at elderly disturbed patients, who didn't seem to have a clue what was happening to them, and thinking how I longed to be even less aware of what was happening to me as well.

"Beverley, can you come through now, please?" a nurse called from around the doorway. I followed her out into the corridor and into an area where there were several dishevelled beds with rather unclean looking sheets strewn across them. "Lie down on the bed here and I'll be back in a minute for you when they're ready." As she disappeared through another door I tried not to think about who might have been in the bed before me as I lay down on it. A few minutes later I was pushed on the bed into another room where one of my colleagues waited, along with the junior psychiatrist who had admitted me.

"Hi Beverley, how are you?" smiled the anaesthetist I recognised from work.

"Oh, I'm fine, thank you, how are you?" I answered automatically, feeling acutely embarrassed because I clearly wasn't fine at all.

The psychiatrist was standing behind my head at the end of the bed with an electric cable in each hand as I tried desperately hard to blot him, and what he was going to do to me, out of my thoughts.

"I'm going to be sick," I thought from absolute terror, but as the anaesthetic raced up my arm, I drifted away and was otherwise unaware of anything else that happened to me afterwards in that room. When I woke up my head was hurting like hell. I don't remember being taken back in the minibus each time, but after every treatment I was put to bed in a side room back on my own ward to sleep off the effects of the anaesthetic and the headache. Paul would arrive each day after work but I have no memory whatsoever of anything during this period. The ECT caused permanent short-term memory loss. Friends from church visited me but I have no recollection of them. Paul would be allowed to take me out sometimes and he took me to meet friends of his that I had never met, but I couldn't remember ever having met them afterwards. He recalls turning up to find me with dull red circles imprinted on my temples, which he found unsettling.

What it didn't do was wipe out traumatic memories, which might have proved more useful, or cure me of my depression, which remained steadfast. Apart from discovering that I couldn't remember anything from that period in my life after the first dose of ECT, it achieved nothing.

Once again I was released back into society to contemplate where I went next. How was I going to survive like this? How much more could I take? When would I be completely well and why had God left me like this when He had supposedly healed me? Questions neither I, nor anyone else knew the answers to, but I was beginning to realise that God wasn't going to let go of me despite what I did.

I had been at work all day trying to ignore debilitating thoughts that intensified to the point that they became a raging battle in the forefront of my mind and absolutely intolerable. Self-harm would shut them up but only for a day or so. Once again, I'd had enough. Unable to stand a moment more of the noise in my head, I fled the office in a wild frenzy to purchase a large quantity of paracetamol to stop it once and for all. Back at my flat I swallowed 90 tablets. As the hours wore on into the night I grew very sick. Hours of endless vomiting ensued, but the following morning I got up and went to work!

I looked a complete sight when I walked in and was taken straight to A & E, but I was walking and coherent. Although my colleagues didn't know what was wrong with me it was very apparent that I was ill. Once alone, I confessed what I'd taken to the doctor examining me and he arranged the usual blood tests but, when the results came back he told me that he didn't believe me because there was not a trace of paracetamol in my body! It had been the biggest overdose I had ever taken and there was not a trace of it in my blood.

I was angry with God. "Why?" I screamed at Him. "Why are you doing this to me? Why won't you let me die? It's too hard. I can't do this so just let go of me, please!" But I knew from that moment on that He had a purpose for me and I was meant to live. How else had I survived all that I had done to myself over the years if God hadn't got a purpose for my life? I clung to the words that He would complete the good work He had begun in me. I had to believe it for all I was worth. There had to be a reason for this, there just had to.

My GP sent me back to London to Professor Clarke to see if he could make any sense of it, but when he wanted to admit me the church seemed fed up with this decision, as it demonstrated lack of faith on my part again. Nevertheless I was admitted and Paul travelled up to London every day to see me after work.

I didn't have many positive feelings as I had shut down my emotions long since and I certainly didn't know if I would ever be capable of love, but I didn't want Paul to leave me either. There was something about him that made me feel safe; I had never felt safe or been able to trust anybody before, so I had to make sure he was going to be there for me when I came home.

"Paul, are you going to stay with me forever?" I blurted out on one particular visit. I don't think he knew how to reply other than to ask me why I wanted to know all of a sudden. Paul left and I really had no idea as to whether or not he would come back after that, but later that evening he returned.

Paul had brought with him an engagement ring. Before the year was out we were married and expecting a baby. There was suddenly so much to fight for, so much worth getting better for.   Paul arranged for private psychiatric treatment for me throughout the pregnancy, some of which was spent back in hospital under the new psychiatrist's care. People were scared though — could I look after a baby? And, what about love? I wanted this baby and I wanted so much to be able to love and I didn't even know what it felt like.

Nicholas was born on 7 May 1991. As I held him in my arms for the first time I felt my heart would burst with love for him. I was so amazed to find that my heart was even capable as it stirred for the first time. "Thank you Jesus," I cried. "Thank you for saving me, thank you for giving me Paul and thank you for this miracle as well, for giving me a son." At last stability seemed to be within reach.

Sixteen months later, God brought along another miracle for us and we called him Jonathon James.

Paul and I moved house and joined the country church in our new village. In fact we bought a little cottage next door-but-one to the vicarage — a safe place. I loved being next to the church and the security that seemed to offer.

During our time at the cottage I started cake baking, mainly for the boys but it developed eventually into a thriving business! I had always had a strong compulsion to cook when in the throes of anorexia but as I began expressing myself more creatively through the cake decorating, I found I was able to channel it into something more than just an obsession with cooking. I went to college one evening a week and studied a City & Guilds in

Sugarcraft and from out of this, a wedding cake business began to flourish through word of mouth.

My faith in God increased and I felt Him calling me and giving me a vision. There was a purpose after all: I was to help others by demonstrating a life dependent on God. I felt called to help young people with mental health issues but didn't know how I was meant to fulfil the calling. I decided the only way I could reach out to others was to work for the church and, in apparent confirmation of this, I was accepted into lay ministry training.

As certain areas of my life improved, the spiritual attack upon me intensified. It was at this point that demonic manifestations became a regular occurrence in our home. My childhood fear returned. It seemed as if I had never been free of the hold they had over me and I was never going to be able to get away. Despite my faith and my involvement in church ministry, we continued to suffer. I didn't know how to fight it and my fear was utterly disabling in itself. I knew it all stemmed from my childhood history in the occult and the fear this had instilled in me. The belief that I could never escape and the absolute hopelessness and futility of trying, was as all consuming as ever. I was depressed again.

Our village church had no experience in spiritual warfare and I felt that, because I worked for the church, people would see me as 'bad' because of the demonic attacks and I felt too ashamed to own up to it. I was also worried because I might not be taken seriously and risked being locked up again. To further complicate matters, I had been conditioned as a child not to say anything 'because people wouldn't understand', so it was never going to be straightforward admitting we needed help with paranormal interference.

Out of desperation, I felt led to Greyfriars, a large town centre church in Reading. I sat quietly at the back during a lively evening service and cried as I felt the presence of the Holy Spirit upon me. I made arrangements to visit the vicar of Greyfriars soon afterwards to ask for help. It came at a time when the attacks were at their peak. When I turned up at the vicarage I was completely terrified. I had a clear red line around my neck, an impression left by a demonic noose that had strangled me when we had attempted deliverance ministry again with some friends of ours.

A couple from the Greyfriars prayer ministry team came to our house, armed just with holy oil and a certainty of their authority and identity in Christ. They anointed the doorframes with oil and walked into each room commanding Satan and all his evil workers to leave in the name of Jesus. As cupboards, doors and windows were opened, the pungent stench of evil that accompanied the breathtakingly icy temperature drops that we had become accustomed to, was exposed and forced to leave. We were all anointed with oil, received communion, the house was prayed through and blessed, and a peace we had never known before descended upon us all.

This marked the beginning of our battle against evil. We didn't understand how Satan continued to have access into our lives and we had no concept whatsoever of the entitlement bestowed upon us the moment we had accepted Jesus into our lives. Despite my faith, and all the courses I had attended as a trainee Lay Reader, I still had no idea what it really meant to be a child of God. I was still scared.

Chapter 14

Walking in Freedom

SOON AFTERWARDS Paul and I attended a Freedom in Christ conference at Greyfriars on how to live free from the bondage of our past. What I heard amazed me! I wondered why I hadn't grasped it before, as I took on board my true identity in Christ and what that really meant, for the first time.

I learnt that, as a Christian, I have authority over Satan. Jesus already has the victory over Satan through his death and resurrection on the cross and therefore, because I am 'in Christ' I have also got authority over Satan (2Cor.5:17). Phil.2:10-11 tells us that at the mere mention of the name of Jesus, *every* knee will bow down and worship.

Why had I been so fearful of Satan then when I had the power within myself to command him to leave me alone?

Because I had remained deceived by him.

I was totally unaware of who I really was as a child of God. My significance was not in being anorectic, but in *being* a child of God. I am significant purely because God loves me and has blessed me with every spiritual blessing in Christ. I was chosen in Him, and adopted as His child through Jesus (Eph.1:3-5). My lack of understanding and knowledge had allowed Satan to hoodwink me and keep me from knowing the truth, and the truth was all I needed to be free. (Jn.8:33.)

I discovered that being frightened in itself had opened a door wide to Satan because there's no fear in Jesus. Rom.8:15 says that I am not a slave to fear anymore because the Spirit I received brought about my adoption.

This realisation changed my whole perspective on life. From there I was able to learn how to live dependent on God. I discovered that controlling my life through starving, as with any addiction, created a barrier between myself and God which allowed Satan access into my life instead. Once he was in he was able to feed his lies into my mind, which I failed to recognise as being part of the spiritual battle I was in. Because I believed the thoughts were mine, or as a consequence of mental illness, they kept me deeply ensnared within my area of dependence. As long as I remained dependent upon something other than God it would form a barrier between myself and God, preventing his Holy Spirit from working effectively within my life and allowing Satan to obscure the truth.

Unfortunately before becoming a Christian I had learnt patterns of living and thinking that were independent of God. Once I became a Christian however, I couldn't just remove all the thoughts and irrational beliefs from my mind without replacing them with a new way of thinking. In Rom. 12:2 Paul said, "Do not conform yourselves to the standards of this world, but let God transform you inwardly by a complete change of your mind. Then you will be able to know the will of God." But I had developed my own patterns of behaviour and thinking in order to cope. Paul refers to these defence mechanisms as 'strongholds' in 2Cor.10:3-5. "It is true that we live in the world, but we do not fight from worldly motives. The weapons we use in our fight are not the world's weapons but God's powerful weapons, which we use to destroy strongholds. We destroy false arguments; we pull down every proud obstacle that is raised against the knowledge of God, we take every thought captive and make it obey Christ."

Learning how to do this, whether with an addiction or not, isn't easy but can certainly be achieved with some hard work. The process I used was a simplistic variant of Cognitive Behaviour Therapy (CBT) based on God's Word. This involves comparing irrational thoughts against what God says and dismissing those belief systems that don't match up. Without removing the old patterns of behaviour first though, it's very difficult to start working on the thoughts. It means taking a huge leap of faith because it's so hard to let go of something you have been dependent on for a long time, although it may be helpful to think of it as a blockage that prevents God from helping until you let go of it.

The first step therefore was to remove all areas of wrongful behaviour which had allowed Satan access into my life. The next step was to confess it and repent – it is the act of repentance that keeps that door shut for good. James 5:16 says 'Therefore confess your sins to each other and pray for each other so that you may be healed. The prayer of a righteous man is powerful and effective.'

I was taken through the Steps to Freedom by a member of the Freedom in Christ team, with three others sitting in as my prayer partners, who themselves went on to take many others through the process following this appointment. It doesn't matter how it's done as long as you understand what can act as a barrier between yourself and God but the simple 'Steps to Freedom in Christ' by Neil Anderson are easy to follow and encompass everything from involvement in the occult, deception and fear, bitterness and unforgiveness, rebellion, pride, sexual sin to generational sin. I've used the same process to lead several others to freedom since.

I suppose it was pretty obvious that I was in a spiritual battle because of my childhood experiences and it might be hard for some people to take on board that we are *all* in a spiritual battle, regardless of whether experiencing demonic manifestations! Many of us develop a whole manner of defence mechanisms and ways of coping with stressful situations, and these are evidence of a spiritual battle because it's a way of living independently of God. I had created numerous ways of coping with the fear I'd felt as a child. In the case of anorexia, there is usually a trigger after a period of prolonged stress, a trigger that is traumatic and anorexia then appears as the final outcome. The catalyst for me had been my parents' divorce.

As with most other cases of anorexia, once I stopped eating all my thoughts became governed by food, starving and weight loss, which subsequently took my mind off what was going on around me. In drugs and alcohol it is a more obvious distraction but in anorexia it's much more complex and some of the effects of starvation aren't actually intentional, or even realised. As the obsession takes hold, the sufferer loses touch with the original trauma and the eating disorder becomes the problem in its place. It then becomes near on impossible to deal with the cause because the original event no longer seems to cause the pain. The disturbed behaviour is now causing its own pain. And so we have a very successful defence mechanism and the creation of a stronghold.

In CBT language: the activating event (A) triggers an irrational belief (B) which causes emotional distress and behaviour (C). A client presents to their GP asking for help with their C, having sometimes lost sight of A. In order to deal with C, the therapist needs to unravel B, which is not always straightforward. If the therapist and client can recognise B and move on to disputing B by replacing the irrational thoughts with more logical beliefs, then it's possible to change C.

What is also interesting in CBT is that C might not be a consequence of the present A, but A has triggered *familiar* irrational beliefs at B, that were formed by a previous activating event in the past. It is the re-emergence of B that has caused the current emotional disturbance.

Therefore if a person can recognise familiar patterns of irrational beliefs and dispute them as they emerge, they can avoid disturbed emotions and dysfunctional behaviour when they face stressful events in the future. It is often very difficult to recognise the irrational beliefs however when you are stuck in distressing emotional behaviour yourself and it can take somebody else to point these out to you before you can see how illogical they are.

Looking at anorexia, why does a normal child suddenly believe they are fat when they are clearly losing enormous amounts of weight to the point of emaciation? Why does she feel the need to starve to be in control? Why does she take huge amounts of laxatives believing that they constantly have to take more even though they haven't eaten anything and certainly aren't constipated? Why does any food swallowed feel so disgusting that it has to be vomited back up? None of these thoughts are rational so why would someone hold on to them to the point of torturing themselves?

Looking at this from a spiritual perspective, traumatic circumstances often cause negative patterns of thinking and behaviour — and Satan gains access through this thinking and starts to feed his own lies into the mind. You believe the thoughts must be true because they appear to be your own. As you accept them as your own, they become normal (despite being totally irrational) and you believe them. You dare not let go of them for fear of losing control. But they are not your own thoughts. They are totally illogical and cause isolation and distraction from God, which is exactly what Satan wants to achieve. Unlike with conventional CBT, the irrational beliefs can be disputed with God's Word. If you believe God is absolute truth, it makes it very simple to reject a belief that doesn't hold up against what God says is true. For example, I could not possibly be a useless failure because in Phil.4:13 it says I can do all things through Christ who strengthens me! In CBT you would dispute the irrational belief that you were a useless failure by telling yourself that whilst you may have failed in one area, you haven't failed in all areas. God's Word is much more powerful than this kind of rationalisation and brings ultimate freedom from negative patterns of thinking that can be sustained.

It would be naïve to suggest that someone with complex problems can simply confess and repent in order to experience an immediate transformation (although in some people this has been the case). Repentance paves the way before the work can actually begin. Repentance removes the barriers between you and God, but in order to keep the barriers down you have to change your behaviour and your belief system.

God has already given us freedom but it is our responsibility to choose to walk in freedom. (Gal.5:1.)

Changing our disturbed behaviour is a choice we can make and we have to exercise this choice, alongside recognising and changing our irrational belief systems by *renewing our minds.*   If we can then recognise familiar patterns of irrational thinking as they arise in the future, and know how to dispute the lies on an ongoing basis, we can live free of disturbed emotions and self destructive behaviour.

Chapter 15

Flashbacks

FLASHBACKS TO TRAUMATIC EXPERIENCES can be traumatic in themselves as you keep on re-living the feelings that were sustained at the time. They can be triggered by something someone says, or by seeing or hearing something that triggers a memory. Sometimes just experiencing a similar emotion to that experienced during the original event may trigger a flashback. Flashbacks can be very intense and literally like re-living the incident all over again.

My flashbacks often ran into each other and my only way of coping with the overwhelming images and emotions was to completely shut everything down. It seemed impossible to stop them with any form of distraction, other than by self harm or to blank everything out.

The following scene was triggered when I was asked an intimate question in therapy. Although the question in itself didn't particularly take me by surprise, my reaction to it did. The question was harmless enough on a conscious level, but it must have triggered something within me on a subconscious level.

"I want my daddy!" I suddenly blurted out.

"What did you just say?" David questioned, cautiously. I had heard it too, but I was as surprised as he was. It was followed by a sense of nothingness, silence, as I shut down.

Why had I said that? The words uttered had been spoken by a child; one that appeared to be no part of me. I had not even been thinking anything along the lines of needing my dad, so where had the words come from? I curled up in the chair, as my mind also seemed to fold in on itself; the words spoken and swallowed up by the ensuing silence.

"Beverley, what's going through your mind right now? Do you want to talk about it?"

I didn't know what I was thinking because a gaping emptiness within my mind overtook the power to reason, to think. My mind had become overloaded and replaced by a destitute state of being.

"Where did you say you were going this week?" An empty stillness. I'd escaped.

"How are the boys getting on at the moment? Is school okay?" David was distracting me, carefully steering me back into my conscious mind. "Did you say you were doing something nice this weekend with them?"

"Yes." It seemed like a voice from a very long way away.

"Where did you say you were going?" he persisted. Slowly and nervously, I responded to the questions as I felt my way back.

"That's nice!" he smiled.

"Yes." A half smile. Eyes half open. A strange, heavy feeling remained, but it was safe and I was back to the present moment again.

'Shutting down' is not done on a conscious level but seems to be a learnt pattern of coping developed to combat extreme stress. When I was about ten years old I used to curl up in a ball on the top shelf of the airing cupboard and shut the doors behind me. I didn't understand what I was doing then but I had in fact developed a successful coping mechanism. As an adult, when stress became overwhelming, the same instinct to curl up and shut down kicked in.

In the situation described above, I had no desire for my dad to protect me at that point in my conscious mind. Deep down inside me however was obviously an unsatisfied desire for love and nurture.

As the brain shuts down further, breathing patterns begin to change, becoming deeper and slower. It's almost like a waking sleep because, whilst still being aware of surroundings and noises, the body feels heavy and everything appears to be happening at a distance. If someone were to talk to you at this point, you would hear the voice but it may seem like too much physical effort is required to respond, perhaps as if under the influence of drugs. Everything feels like it is happening in slow motion and every step seems to require enormous effort and concentration.

'Shutting down' is a form of dissociation, a coping mechanism adopted in times of persistent extreme stress. Anorexia is another form of dissociation and one that is very effective because as more weight is lost, the part of the brain that deals with emotions seems to become less effective and so a real physical state of dissociation is triggered. As the weight goes back on and the brain begins to function more normally again, the individual begins to feel as if they're losing control, and it is this feeling of losing control that causes many anorectics to relapse. Control is about feeling safe when life has felt out of control and very much unsafe.

It's very easy to feed lies into the mind of the vulnerable, especially one whose life has been dominated by the occult. The anorectic patient responds to voices or thoughts that say she isn't good enough unless she loses more weight. But these are not psychotic voices, no matter how irrational they seem. Doesn't everybody hear voices of some kind but does that mean we are all psychotic to some greater or lesser degree? How many of us experience doubting, nagging voices that tell us we are not good enough, or that someone doesn't like us? These thoughts are all destructive but we usually accept them as our own. But we are all in a spiritual battle and Satan's aim is to tempt us to take our eyes off Jesus by any means he can. If he can destroy lives by encouraging us to rely on self defeating beliefs and behaviours, so much the better. Satan is the deceiver, the prince of lies and in 1Pet.5:8 we are told that he roams the earth like a roaring lion ready to devour and destroy. But look at the previous verse: 'Leave all your worries with Him, because He cares for you.'

God knows that we will be in danger if we do not cast our worries and anxieties upon Him, and this is actually a command given in order that we do not fall victim to Satan. Through anxiety and fear comes self reliance, and through self reliance comes distraction away from God, and His truth – that we have *already* been given freedom.

If we have already been given our freedom, we should be experiencing freedom in our lives. So how do we do that? By keeping our eyes fixed on Jesus and refusing to listen to the lies of the enemy. See Heb.12:1-3 'Therefore since we are surrounded by such a great cloud of witnesses, let us throw off everything that hinders and the sin that so easily entangles, and let us run with perseverance the race marked out for us. Let us fix our eyes on Jesus, the author and perfector of our faith, who for the joy set before him endured the cross, scorning its shame and sat down at the right hand of the throne of God.   Consider him who endured such opposition from sinful men, so that you will not grow weary and lose heart.'

In the process of renewing our minds and changing the way we see ourselves, we should renounce the irrational belief by claiming the truth in scripture. One way of doing this is in the form of a simple prayer, a 'stronghold buster'. (examples can be seen in chapter 15) Apparently it takes about six weeks to form a habit and equally, 40 days to break it and renew your mind. The Bible tells us that God often prepared people over a 40 day period, from Noah (40 days of rain), Moses (40 days on Mount Sinai), David (facing Goliath's 40 day challenge), Elijah (40 days energy from one meal) and Jesus himself, who spent 40 days in the wilderness before beginning his ministry. So 40 days is clearly also a spiritually significant period of time.

It would be realistic to accept that certain areas are bound to remain sensitive because we all have weaknesses whether or not we have addictive personalities, suffer from an eating disorder, or have suffered from debilitating trauma of some kind. Paul talks about the 'thorn in his side' in 2Cor.12:7-9: 'To keep me from becoming conceited because of these surpassingly great revelations, there was given me a thorn in my flesh, a messenger of Satan, to torment me. Three times I pleaded with the Lord to take it away from me. But he said to me, "My grace is sufficient for you, for my power is made perfect in weakness."'

Satan knows our weaknesses too, but once we have shut all the doors that allowed him in we are able to put on the armour of God (Eph.6:10-18) to protect ourselves from his attacks.

I was healed from anorexia in 1987 after I came out of the secure unit. It was to my utter amazement when I finally turned the corner. God gave me the will to live and the 'promise' of a healing which I believed wholeheartedly. At the time, although I thought I should have been completely and miraculously healed immediately, I continued to suffer with immense difficulties that conflicted with this healing and made no sense of it. When I look back now I can see that I had been given that healing in one form, but I still had to work through the problem of undoing my irrational beliefs and renewing my mind. As I sought God in this, He was able to come through with the provision of a deeper healing.

I see this as trusting God, turning to Him and believing that I would be healed, even when things seemed to be suggesting otherwise. Despite the recovery from anorexia that eventually followed, life remained extremely tough for a considerable period afterwards. I'm sure that a failure to look to God at this point would have resulted in an unfulfilled promise and I may still have died had I not believed in God's provision for fulfilling that promise. Philippians 1:6 says: 'He who began a good work in you will carry it on to completion.' It was during this period that these words were particularly poignant.

When Daniel prayed to God and fasted over a 21 day period about the future of his people, the angel made it obvious to him that Daniel's prayer had been heard by God on the first day of his fast but resistance to the answer in the spiritual realm had delayed God's answer for the full 21 days. This shows the importance of 'praying through' and persisting until we receive the assurance of answered prayer. God's way of dealing with us while we are at this stage is often to bring us to a point of total dependence upon Him. Sometimes it can seem as if God is not with us when we pray out in that wilderness place and seem to receive no answer.

I know of someone who prayed for the healing of her daughter for 25 years before that prayer was answered. Although she rejoiced in that healing when it came, she couldn't help but wonder why it took so long. Although her daughter was a Christian, it was only when she understood her identity in Christ and exercised her own authority and responsibility to shut all the doors that had been opened to Satan in her life, that she was able to experience healing.

In order then to renew the mind it is imperative to find the underlying lie. This is usually easier with the help of someone else because the irrational belief often appears to be true to the individual, no matter how illogical it may appear to somebody else. I believed so many lies about myself, from thinking that I was hopeless and worthless, to thinking that I was only good enough if I weighed a certain weight, and it took a lot of time and encouragement from others to be able to see that the beliefs I'd held for so long were completely untrue. It's because I've experienced such a depth of healing and revelation in this area that I feel so passionate about helping other people unravel these debilitating negative thought patterns and show them how to replace them with God's absolute truth in order to renew the mind.

Chapter 16

Feed my Sheep

I FELT VERY CLEARLY that God was leading me into putting this call into practice by offering to care for individuals within our home, as had been done for me. I had been working in the Freedom in Christ UK office for a couple of years by then and we were still busy preparing our first host church (my own home church) who were going to pilot the scheme by taking in a young woman who was being tube-fed in hospital. I was busy writing the guidelines and working out a programme when God brought Laura to us instead.

Laura had written to me a year earlier, desperate for help and suicidal. She continued to write from hospital throughout the year until she phoned one day out of the blue asking if she could come to stay immediately. It transpired that she had left the hospital for the weekend on leave but had overdosed on her medication, for which the hospital had put her on enforced leave for a week 'to contemplate her actions'. Her parents felt unable to cope with her illness and so she had to find somewhere else to go. Having only met her once briefly, when she was heavily sedated, I didn't really know her other than through her many letters but God had already placed her on my heart. We didn't have a spare room and I couldn't find anybody else willing or able to take her in.

I knew it was right to agree to her coming nevertheless as I felt God had been leading us in this direction for some time. So the very next day Paul and I drove to Kent and brought her back to Reading with us. Her mother handed over her medication from the hospital and Laura didn't appear to have anything else on her. We made up a bed for her in the dining room.

As well as having anorexia and bulimia, Laura was addicted to prescription medications and alcohol, and was a compulsive self-harmer.

When I took her with me to the FIC office the following day, she was very drowsy so we made up a bed for her on a couple of chairs. Telling me that she hadn't slept all night, she then slept most of the day and avoided eating any lunch.

Later that evening, having persuaded Laura to have some fruit juice because she hadn't eaten lunch, I went into the dining room to find her sitting on the floor writing a letter to her mother. I sat down beside her and suddenly noticed a bottle of pills in an open bag in front of her. As I reached for them she went into a total panic, begging me to give them back to her. I later discovered that she had smuggled these into the house by concealing them in the socks that she was wearing. As I sat there on the floor with her, holding onto the remaining bottle and trying to reason with her, I noticed a large wet puddle under the bed. When questioned, Laura immediately seemed very ashamed and told me that I would kill her and send her home if I knew what she'd done. I was dismayed to find that she had poured the fruit juice out over the carpet under the bed instead of drinking it.

All she could think about however, was the fact that I had taken her pills. Jonathon had a friend over for tea that evening, the mother was due anytime and I still hadn't actually fed them anything, so I decided to call for some support. Phil Cole, who was the pastoral director at my church, came immediately with his wife Shirley and were rather taken aback by this forlorn figure curled up on the floor, repeatedly begging for her pills. I left them to try to deal with the situation whilst I sorted the boys out with some food.

Phil and Shirley were at a loss as to what to do to help move Laura on and so called Steve Goss at FIC for advice. Despite the fact that she was so heavily drugged that she could barely open her eyes, we all then worked together to encourage her to exercise her own responsibility and authority as a Christian. By 11.30 p.m. Steve had lead her through the Steps to Freedom and we finally reached a turning point. She looked up and smiled, all the angst from earlier that evening gone from her face.

Because Laura had been so heavily sedated, it was still necessary to go through the process again a couple of days later when she could really confront issues and repent with a clear state of mind. She came home eight hours later telling everybody that Jesus had set her free! Her face was radiant and her smile was enough to convince anyone that something miraculous really had happened. Laura's parents came to visit a few days later and as her mother put her arms around her, she whispered to her that she had got her daughter back at last, bringing tears to my eyes. Her mother didn't have to wait to hear what Laura had to tell her, she could see for herself that something had changed.

Despite all of this, Laura still had to learn to walk in freedom and it wasn't easy. She was addicted to drugs and she wanted to start reducing her dependence on them. Whilst this was something she wanted to achieve herself, at times the thoughts in her mind were telling her how good it felt when she took them. She genuinely longed for them at times and struggled so much with the craving that it was hard work convincing her at times that she could take a stand against it. She would renounce the thoughts, only to find them back again later and she would question whether it would ever be possible to overcome her dependence.

I was extremely careful to keep her medication locked away, and all the kitchen knives and scissors were hidden. I always took her shopping with me in order to monitor what she bought and made sure that when I left her in the care of someone else, that they also stayed with her. Having written myself guidelines, and thinking I knew all the tricks possible because I had done them all myself, I rather naïvely thought I could avoid them.

Laura went to visit a friend of mine one afternoon. While they were out she insisted that she needed to visit a chemist and even managed to convince my friend that she needed to buy a new razor to shave her legs. My friend never thought for a minute that she had any ulterior motive and forgot to mention the visit to the chemist to me. Laura returned home and when the going got tough a couple of days later, she cut herself.

Laura stayed with us for ten months in total, during which time she was eventually eating normally, had stopped self-harming and drinking, and had stopped self medicating. She returned home to live with her parents and was so full of all God had done for her that she then started helping several of her own friends. She still struggled with the desire for drugs but she was determined to renew her mind completely and 18 months after leaving us, she was still working on new prayers she had written herself to deal with other problem areas. This was not because she was struggling anymore than anyone else but because she recognised the fact that taking every thought captive in obedience to Christ is an ongoing process.

Lesley was a compulsive eater and the most appalling self-harmer I have ever come across. A year after Laura had started the programme, Lesley turned up to stay with us following surgery for a deep stab wound to her stomach that she had inflicted upon herself. She had lost five pints of blood, coming very close to death and after seven years of self-harming, she wanted to be free of it. She weighed 24.5 stones and was covered from head to toe with horrific scars.

I have to admit to feeling very scared of her and the first night she was in our home, Paul and I sat up all night praying, feeling it was unsafe to sleep with her in the house with the children. Although I knew that God had brought her to us, I spent the night praying along the lines of "Lord you brought her here, but this is too much and I know that I can't do this on my own, or in my own strength, so if you want her free, you'll have to do it!" which is of course the only way it could be done anyway.

Lesley returned home after going through the Steps to Freedom over the course of a weekend and managed very well on her own for a month or so. It then became apparent that the self destructive thought patterns she was familiar with were too much for her to fight on her own without support, and she returned to stay with us.

One of the things we encouraged was to establish as normal a daily routine as possible, which involved a variety of activities and included some voluntary work in the community to mimic a normal working day. For the first six weeks though Lesley worked on her first prayer to renew her mind and needed plenty of support while the feelings were intense and raw. This is when it's essential to take a step of faith with the eating, or other addictive behaviour, because thinking that it's a waste of time and nothing is ever going to change, is normal. In fact the thoughts can be even more intense during these six weeks as Satan knows he's about to lose this ground in your life if you complete it. Once the first six weeks have been completed, it is possible to see a radical change in thinking.

Lesley lost about five stone and began to feel better about herself, although she had many slip-ups during her time with us. Due to the aggressiveness of her self-harm, (which in addition to stabbing herself with carving knives included overdosing, cutting herself with broken crockery and glass, scalding herself with boiling water, and burning herself with irons) it was necessary for her to go into hospital on several occasions.

After one episode of self harm she was Sectioned and admitted to a psychiatric secure unit. As she was staying with us, I was involved in her care plan whilst she was an in-patient. It felt very strange to walk on to a secure unit again and, even more so, to be part of the team rather than to be on the receiving end - which I hoped was an encouragement to Lesley as well. I was able to continue praying with her on a daily basis on the ward and her consultant was very interested in what we were doing, saying that many of his patients would benefit from it!

They told me that they had never seen such severe self-harm as they witnessed with Lesley. On one occasion she tied a sock around her neck so tightly that it had embedded into the flesh so deeply that it became invisible. The doctor initially thought she was having an anaphylactic shock reaction to her drugs due to the facial swelling and he left to look up her medication in her notes. Something must have alerted one of the nurses who rushed back to the room, by which time her face was a dark navy colour, and when she tilted her head backwards they discovered the sock that was strangulating her.

Following on from this incident and while Lesley was still in the hospital, it dawned on me that Lesley struggled with the feeling that she actually *wanted* to self harm (as Laura had wanted her drugs). Once the thought was in her head, she wanted it so badly that she didn't care about the consequences - in fact even the consequences were exciting to her. I felt inspired to write a Crisis Management Plan which focused on the fact that this feeling was a lie and that other thoughts or behaviour always precipitated this feeling. We were able to trace it back to discover that before she felt like this, she was dwelling on other thoughts such as that she would never be good enough, never be able to live a normal life, was different, ugly, useless — typical lies for many, not just those struggling with an eating disorder or self-harm. Therefore working on these thoughts the moment she was aware of them, by having prayers written in preparation and eventually learnt, would help her to fight them and to take the thoughts captive the moment they came into her head.

I also realised that there was another step prior to this one which would trigger off these first thoughts. Thinking and dwelling on the attractiveness and appeal of self-harm, as well as the saving up and hiding of implements to use later, would open a doorway to Satan. What God revealed to me here was confirmed in the passage in Matthew 5 on adultery: "You have heard that it was said, 'Do not commit adultery.' But I tell you that anyone who looks at a woman lustfully has already committed adultery with her in his heart" (v.27-28).

Most people are familiar with this passage, but have you considered the fact that if someone has already committed any act of sin in their mind, then surely the *thoughts themselves* need renouncing, as with sins actually committed? Therefore if Lesley is so much as *thinking* about self-harm, she has committed the act already in her mind and has opened a doorway to Satan, without actually having done it in the physical sense. So, if she does not renounce the thoughts at this stage, this will lead on to her thinking the usual lies about herself and her self-worth, before this then leads on to the full blown thought that she *wants* to self-harm. Even at this stage, the use of absolute truth as a ready prepared weapon, her sword of the spirit, could be implemented to cast the thought aside.

I wrote her a crisis prayer for such an occasion based on Heb.9:11-28 and Rom.6:12-13. "I renounce the lie that I want to self harm and accept the truth that only the blood of Christ will cleanse my conscience from acts that lead to death. I choose to offer my body only to you Lord God as an instrument of righteousness. Thank you that you have heard my voice and will save me, amen."

Lesley then discovered that this plan worked and she was able to stop self-harming, usually putting an end to things long before she reached the point of actually wanting to do it. After eight long months she was well on her way and finally able to get a job and drop her benefits, whilst we continued to support her as she found her feet.

Unfortunately, not long after getting a job and during the process of looking for her own accommodation, Lesley decided again that self-harm was more appealing than moving forwards with her life and chose not to dispute this lie. When she left us, we were left in a state of utter exhaustion and overwhelming sadness. I knew that the Lord had wanted to bring Lesley to us so why had she suddenly changed her mind? Had we failed her and God in some way? What had gone wrong, as after all, she had been so close to completing the programme and being able to take responsibility for herself? Did she actually want to, we wondered? She had seemed to at times.

One of our intercessors pointed out when we were praying together after the event, that the outcome was always going to be God's, not ours. All that mattered was that we did what we had been called to do, and the rest would be up to Him. He pointed out that God is big enough to overcome any mistakes we had made in order to bring about the outcome that He had already planned.

It is also important to remember that God gave us all choice. He gives us every opportunity to make the right choice and to follow Him, but making that choice is our own responsibility.

Despite the choices Lesley made, she is still free in Christ; she is still able to choose truth and has been given everything she needs to walk free in Christ.

Fifteen years after moving on from the church where Paul and I met, I happened to meet a lady through the Reading Christian Network at the FIC office. I had not recognised her name and did not even recognise her face when I saw her, but she looked at me for a few moments before asking if I was the same person she had visited in hospital all those years earlier. She had visited me several times while I was having ECT — which is why I had no memory of her — and had prayed regularly for me over the years. She was so moved to see me well that it brought tears to her eyes, as it did to mine when I discovered that she had been praying for me for twenty years with no feedback as to how I was doing.

Sometimes, we are not so lucky to see someone healed after expending so much time with the Lord praying for them, but we never know the effect of our prayers in the heavenlies, as with Daniel and his 21 day fast. But we need to have faith because a seed may have been planted in someone that may take years of watering to come to fruition. It is a shame when you don't see the outcome yourself but God's timing is perfect.

I decided to go away on retreat to pray for wisdom as to the way forwards. After Lesley left us, she set herself on fire and spent weeks in a burns unit, nearly losing her leg. It all seemed to have been for nothing and we didn't feel like going through it again with anyone else. I went away with a heavy heart.

On the second day of my retreat I was sitting in the chapel praying on my own when I saw a vision of Jesus cooking fish on the edge of the sea whilst the disciples were out in their boat fishing. Peter looked up and recognised Jesus and came wading through the water towards Him. The vision faded but I felt God was telling me to go and look up the passage. I said back to him, "Hang on a minute, I'm praying for my children and I want to know what your will is here for us as a family..." God's response to me was still to read the passage in John, but I carried on arguing with him over the relevance of the vision when I was praying about whether my children would be okay and what I was meant to be doing, when I felt God say, "Get down on your knees." I got down and instantly felt a rush of colour and 'living water' flowing down across my head and out through my heart, like a river was rushing over and through me. I heard the words, "The boys will be fine."

I rushed back to my room and looked up the passage. It was from John 21 beginning at verse 1. "Jesus appeared again to his disciples, by the Sea of Tiberias. It happened this way: Simon Peter, Thomas, Nathaniel, the sons of Zebedee and two other disciples were together. 'I'm going out to fish,' Simon Peter told them and they said 'We'll go with you.' So they went out and got into the boat, but that night they caught nothing. Early in the morning, Jesus stood on the shore, but the disciples did not realize that it was Jesus. He called out to them, 'Friends, haven't you any fish?' 'No,' they answered. He said, 'Throw your net on the right side of the boat and you will find some.' When they did, they were unable to haul the net in because of the large number of fish. Then the disciple whom Jesus loved said to Peter, 'It is the Lord!' As soon as Simon Peter heard him say this, he wrapped his outer garment around him and jumped into the water. The other disciples followed in the boat, towing the net full of fish, for they were not far from shore about a hundred yards. When they landed, they saw a fire of burning coals there with fish on it, and some bread. Jesus said to them, 'Bring some of the fish you have just caught.' Simon Peter climbed aboard and dragged the net ashore. It was full of large fish, but even with so many the net was not torn. Jesus said to them, 'Come and have breakfast.' None of the disciples dared ask him, 'Who are you?' They knew it was the Lord. Jesus came, took the bread and gave it to them and did the same with the fish. This was now the third time Jesus appeared to his disciples after he was raised from the dead.

When they had finished eating, Jesus said to Simon Peter, 'Simon son of John, do you truly love me more than these?' 'Yes, Lord,' he said, 'you know that I love you.' Jesus said 'Feed my lambs.' Again Jesus said, 'Simon son of John, do you truly love me?' He answered, 'Yes Lord, you know that I love you.' Jesus said 'Take care of my sheep.' The third time he said to him, 'Simon, son of John, do you love me?' Peter was hurt because Jesus asked him the third time, 'Do you love me?' He said, 'Lord you know all things, you know that I love you.' Jesus said, 'Feed my sheep.'"

Upon reading this, I knew what God was saying to me. The Lord was calling us to feed his sheep also, and He had reassured me that the boys would be fine. Deep in my heart though, I also knew that God was telling me that it would happen in a new way to the way we'd been working. I didn't know what this meant and, to be honest, I didn't want to acknowledge this part of what I knew He was saying. It meant waiting to see what God was going to do next and, being the impetuous person I am, waiting is not one of my strong points!

Chapter 17

Stronghold Busters

SOME STRONGHOLDS may have a greater hold on the mind than others and more work is needed to break them down. Here is a more in-depth formula for breaking through lies from the Freedom in Christ teaching material:

1. Identify the lie (a lie is a way of thinking which contradicts what God says in the Bible about us). Try to ignore feelings at this stage and submit entirely to the truth. The feelings follow later.

   I was once told "you don't feel your way into good behaviour; you behave your way into good feelings!" and I've never forgotten it.

2. Search for as many verses as you can that state the truth and write them down.

3. Write a prayer based on the following: 'I renounce the lie that...... I believe the truth that......' using several of the verses from scripture that you have written down.

4. Read the passages and say the prayer every day for 40 days, continuously telling yourself that God is

truth and that if He has said it, it must be true for you too. It is God's job to be truth — your job is to believe the truth!

Another really important thing to remember when writing this prayer is to thank God and to praise Him even when you don't feel like it. I believe that this alone can turn whole situations around. Thanking God for what He has given us, even when there doesn't seem anything to be thankful for, releases the power of the Holy Spirit into that situation in order to bring about healing and turn it around.

Corrie Ten Boom writes about this in her book *The Hiding Place*, as does Merlin R Carothers in his book *Bringing Heaven Into Hell*. Both write of different situations whereby it would be impossible for most of us to want to thank God. It was through thanking God however, that both have been able to write about blessings coming out of terrible situations.

The following is the first stronghold buster that was written for me before I learnt to do it myself:

1. **LIE**: 'How good/acceptable/lovable I am is based on what I look like and since my body is unacceptable, I am not lovable.'

2. **TRUTH**:

Psalm 139:13:

'For you created every part of me; you put me together in my mother's womb. I praise you because I am fearfully and wonderfully made; your works are wonderful, I know that full well. When my bones were being formed, carefully put together in my mother's womb, when I was growing there in secret, you knew that I was there — you saw me before I was born. All the days allotted to me were recorded in your book before any of them came to be.'

Therefore, God was very much involved when my body was formed and He did a very good job!

Hebrews 10:19-23:

'We have, then, my brothers, complete freedom to go into the Most Holy Place by means of the death of Jesus. He opened for us a new way, a living way, through the curtain — that is, through his own body. We have a great priest in charge of the house of God. So let us come near to God with a sincere heart and sure faith, with hearts that have been purified from a guilty conscience and with bodies washed with clean water. Let us hold on firmly to the hope we profess, because we can trust God to keep his promise.'

Therefore, even if I have messed up, my body is now washed with pure water and is completely acceptable to God.

Matthew 6:25-27

'This is why I tell you not to be worried about the food and drink you need in order to stay alive, or about clothes for your body. After all, isn't life worth more than food? And isn't the body worth more than clothes? Look at the birds flying around: they do not sow seeds, gather a harvest and put it in barns; yet your Father in heaven takes care of them! Aren't you worth much more than birds? Can any of you live a bit longer by worrying about it?'

Therefore, the appearance of my body is not what is important.   Life is more important than food.   I am worthy to God.

Colossians 2:20 - Col.3:3

'You have died with Christ and are set free from the ruling spirits of the universe. Why then do you live as though you belonged to this world? Why do you obey such rules as "Don't handle this,"   "Don't taste that," "Don't touch the other"? All these refer to things which become useless once they are used; they are only man-made rules and teachings. Of course such rules appear to be based on wisdom in their forced worship of angels and false humility, and severe treatment of the body; but they have no real value in controlling physical passions. You have been raised to life with Christ, so set your hearts on the things that are in heaven, where Christ sits on his throne at the right-hand side of God. Keep your minds fixed on things there, not on things here on earth. For you have died, and your life is hidden with Christ in God.'

Therefore, staying in control by starving isn't going to work! Focusing on God is what matters.

1 Thessalonians 5:23-24

'May the God who gives us peace make you holy in every way and keep your whole being — spirit, soul and body — free from every fault at the coming of our Lord Jesus Christ. He who calls you will do it because he is faithful.'

Therefore, my body is sanctified through and through and completely blameless and perfect in Christ.

3. **PRAYER:** Based on the above truths, I prayed the following prayer for forty days:

'Thank you Lord, that you were there when my body was formed and that you took great care over it. Thank you that I am fearfully and wonderfully made.

I know that in my past there were lots of things that might have messed this up, but even so, you now declare that my body is washed with pure water and is completely acceptable to you. My body is sanctified through and through and completely blameless and perfect in Christ.

I renounce the lie that my body is in any way unacceptable as a result of my past experiences and joyfully accept it back as a gift from you. Thank you that it is clean, lovely and beautiful in your eyes and you are Truth.

I renounce the deception that what I look like is the most important thing and I choose to set my mind on things above. Amen.'

Once a stronghold is broken it remains dealt with so don't be deceived into thinking that you need to do anymore than this. Remember however that Satan will always attack in areas where we are vulnerable. You will occasionally get the same familiar thoughts tempting you, but as soon as the thought comes into your head you can reject it immediately.

You are in a stronger place than previously and you won't need to give into the lie. Just ignore it and carry on.

If you have received Christ as your Saviour, He has already set you free through His victory over sin and death on the cross. Satan knows you have authority over him in Christ, but he doesn't want *you* to know it. He is a liar and the only way he can have power over you is if you believe his lies. His aim is to win the battle for your mind. Remember, Satan only has power over you if you believe the lie. Expose the lie by getting it out in the open then choose the truth, and the power of that lie is broken.

Believing this area to be crucial in healing, I began praying earnestly that God would show me how to put this into such a way that I could share with others. God answered that prayer through the following situation:

One evening Paul and I were downstairs reading and preparing a bible study. I really enjoyed the time we spent on this together and felt a sense of God's peace as I went to bed, which was still with me when I got up the following morning. It was a beautiful encounter with God that remained with me for the entire day.

The following day when I awoke, I was disappointed to discover that the amazing feeling of peace that I'd experienced the previous day had gone. Despite time spent in prayer, it did not return. I knew that God's peace is always sufficient and is always there; I knew that was the Truth. I knew that it had not actually gone but I was very flustered as to why I was not able to *feel* it. I continued to pray about it all morning until I realised what God was showing me.

God's peace *is* always there. It says so in His Word. It is the Truth. We must not rely on our feelings or our circumstances, which change from day to day, because God's Word is always the same and never changes. Therefore, we have to choose to accept and believe His Truth even when we can't see it or feel it. This is an act of faith.

God had allowed me to experience His peace as a feeling for one day and had then withdrawn that feeling the following day. This did not mean that His peace was not there, or any less powerful than it had been the previous day, because His Word states that it is always there and always sufficient. God's peace is not a *feeling*, it is the Truth. I was confused into thinking that peace was an emotional state, and if I was right with God and there was nothing to block it, I should always be able to feel it.

The Oxford English Dictionary tells us that peace is 'Freedom from, or cessation of war; a treaty securing this, a civil order as secured by law.' I was surprised to read that it doesn't tell us anywhere that it is a pleasant feeling! God's Word tells us in John 14:27 'Peace is what I leave with you; it is my own peace that I give you. I do not give it as the world does. Do not be worried and upset; do not be afraid.' And in John 16:33: 'You will have peace by being united to me.' Rom:5:1-2: 'Now that we have been put right with God through faith, we have peace with God through our Lord Jesus Christ.'

Jesus is our treaty and through Him we have God's peace. We are also told not to be worried, upset or afraid and to depend on God because He will deliver us from all our troubles. As He knows more about our troubles than we ourselves do, He must also know the best way of dealing with them. What good can be achieved by worrying then? Worrying and not trusting God is to be self reliant as opposed to God reliant, which gives Satan access to our minds again. Whilst this is hard to do, it is simply a case of believing truth and not basing the truth upon our own feelings - which cannot be relied upon.

Therefore, 'fill your minds with those things that are good and that deserve praise: things that are true, noble, right, pure, lovely and honourable. Put into practice what you learnt and received from me, both from my words and from my actions, and the God who gives us peace will be with you.' (Phil.4:8.)

God gave me another illustration while I was pondering all of this. I was sitting in my car at the traffic lights in heavy traffic about to cross over the motorway, when I noticed a bird fluttering furiously directly in front of me and only a few feet off the ground. It was staying completely still in the air despite flapping its wings frantically. I was mesmerised by this little bird's activity and felt that God was showing me that by flapping our wings in our lives like this, by rushing around, panicking and worrying, we will only stay still and will achieve nothing.

Then the bird stopped flapping and rose smoothly into the air, gliding on those wings as it found an air current. In the same way, if we can learn to depend on God, to accept His Truth instead of believing all the lies that we hold on to, and decide to take that step of faith, we can move forwards in our lives in a new way. That may mean eating, when everything within us is screaming not to, or putting a stop to something else that our body or mind craves.

Jesus is the only one who can satisfy our deepest needs. Food does not satisfy us completely, and certainly abstinence from it does not. In Psalm 107, we read, 'They were hungry and thirsty and had given up all hope. Then in their trouble they called to the Lord, and He saved them from their distress .... They must thank the Lord for His constant love, for the wonderful things he did for them. He satisfies those who are thirsty and fills the hungry with good things .... He brought them out of their gloom and darkness and broke their chains in pieces. They must thank the Lord for His constant love .... Some were fools, suffering because of their sins and because of their evil; they couldn't stand the sight of food and were close to death. Then in their trouble they called to the Lord, and He saved them from their distress. He healed them with His command and saved them from the grave. They must thank the Lord for His constant love, for the wonderful things He did for them.'

It is not only important to turn to God for help, to repent of our sins, but also to *thank* Him for the wonderful things He does for us!

Satan is striving to achieve a constant state of confusion in order to prevent us from recognising truth. It is tempting to think, whilst feeling so tormented and wretched, that you are dealing with this on your own, but this is a lie. Returning to my illustration about not being able to feel God's peace, you have to make a decision to choose to believe truth. We must not depend upon our feelings because whether we can feel God's presence or not, He *is* there and He is absolute truth. His truth never changes. All we have to do is take responsibility for believing it.

We read in Matthew 11:28-29: 'Come to me, all of you who are tired from carrying heavy loads and I will give you rest. Take my yoke and put it on you and learn from me because I am gentle and humble in spirit and you will find rest.'

Let us re-cap then on how to find freedom and live a life that is dependent on God.

Understand what it actually means to be a child of God, to know your true identity and authority in Christ. Ephesians chapter 1:3-8 says, 'Praise be to the God and Father of our Lord Jesus Christ, who has blessed us in the heavenly realms with every spiritual blessing in Christ. For He chose us in Him before the creation of the world to be holy and blameless in His sight. In love He predestined us to be adopted as His sons through Jesus Christ, in accordance with His pleasure and will – to the praise of His glorious grace, which He has freely given us in the one He loves. In him we have redemption through His blood, the forgiveness of sins, in accordance with the riches of God's grace that He lavished on us with all wisdom and understanding.'

Find someone who will pray with you. James 5:13-16 says 'Is any of you in trouble? He should pray. Is anyone happy? Let him sings songs of praise. Is any one of you sick? He should call the elders of the church to pray over him and anoint him with oil in the name of the Lord. And the prayer offered in faith will make the sick person well; the Lord with raise him up. If he has sinned, he will be forgiven. Therefore confess your sins to each other and pray for each other so that you may be healed.' A useful tool to use is the Freedom in Christ *Steps to Freedom.*

And finally, work very thoroughly on breaking those strongholds and renewing your mind so you can experience God's freedom from irrational thoughts and dysfunctional emotional behaviour.

Chapter 18

Conclusion

OUR LIVES REMAIN CHANGED since we realised our true identities in Christ.

I am often asked how I cope with the memories I have. I have tried to write this book as openly and as honestly as I can in order to give you a full picture of the horrors of living with an eating disorder, as well the dangers and risks involved in meddling with the occult. I hope by having done so it may help you to understand how a loved one/patient may be feeling. For those of you suffering with any form of mental illness, I hope this gives you hope that a full recovery in Christ is possible. Reading through and sharing my hospital records has probably been the hardest part of this process, but has highlighted even more for me the incredible miracle that God has performed in my life.

Somebody once said to me that I needed to thank God for what happened because He allowed it to happen for a reason. Initially, I struggled with this and felt angry at the suggestion but over the years I have come to see this from a different perspective. I gave it a lot of prayer because I couldn't understand how it could ever be possible but I wanted to grasp it if it were true.

During a conversation with my school friend, Amanda, who became a Christian as a teenager, she happened to say, "I'm really envious of you. Whilst I would never want to go through what you have gone through, you have experienced God in a way I never have. You have experienced two extremes of which I have never known."

So here was something to thank God for! Without those terrifying experiences, I may never have encountered God the way I have done.

With regards to communicating with the dead, I know that Satan is a liar. He wants to destroy lives, destroy families, bring confusion and unhappiness in any way he can. If you get involved in the occult, you are giving him a wide open door to walk in and start trampling all over your mind and your life. Playing with the occult is dangerous and not worth it! I don't believe that dead relatives can communicate with us but I believe that demons surround us all of our lives. They know us intimately. They know our family members intimately. They know our weaknesses and our pain and our loss. They would know exactly how to convince you that they were your dead relatives. They know secrets that you think only you know. They know exactly how to fool you into believing. Satan is after all the ultimate deceiver and prince of lies.

Once you believe that someone you have lost is trying to communicate with you and you keep going back to that medium, that Spiritualist church, that fortune teller, you are being led further away from God and the truth. God says these things are detestable to him. Dt.18:10-13: 'Let no-one be found among you … who practises divination or sorcery, interprets omens, engages in witchcraft, or casts spells, or who is a medium or spiritist, or who consults the dead.

Anyone who does these things is detestable to the Lord and because of these detestable practices, the Lord your God will drive out those nations before you. You must be blameless before the Lord your God.' Lev.20:6: 'I will set my face against the person who turns to mediums and spiritists to prostitute himself by following them, and I will cut him off from his people.'

God isn't just telling us not to practice as a medium, he is telling us not to consult with one at all. Isaiah says this (Is.8:19-20): 'When men tell you to consult mediums and spiritists, who whisper and mutter, should not a people enquire of their God? Why consult the dead on behalf of the living? To the law and to the testimony! If they do not speak according to this word, they have no light of dawn.'

It is wrong purely because He told us not to do it.

I have found much encouragement in the words of Isaiah 66:13: 'As a mother comforts her child, so I will comfort you, and you will be comforted.'

There are days when the pain caused by the memories is so enormous that the temptation is not to eat to control those feelings, but this is my irrational belief system coming into play and if I listen, Satan will have freedom to walk all over my mind. I have to make a choice not to listen to him or give in. At those times I hear God's gentle and firm voice, "You can give up if you want because you have that choice or you can get up and fight this with me." These days I choose to fight, and when the child within me longs to cry out for mummy, I direct those needs towards God because he is not only my Father, my daddy, he is also capable of being my mummy.

God can wave a magic wand and make it all go away if He wanted to but one of the most important things God gave us right back in the beginning was freedom of choice. God gave us choice for a reason. He wants us to choose to believe, choose to have faith, choose to love and choose to trust Him for ourselves so we can have a relationship with Him.

There is ALWAYS hope, whether feeling well or feeling depressed, because God is still there. The Bible does not tell us that the life we choose to live in Christ will be free from adversity, but it is a life of eternity and we can choose to walk in the freedom He has already given us. We need to keep our eyes fixed on Jesus and never stop praising and thanking Him because in doing so, the power of the Holy Spirit is released and we will be blessed and healed. We are not meant to suffer but we will face trials and tribulations, and through them we must *still* thank God because He is there with us.

There is power in His word and if you can learn to depend on it, we can fight every battle – and win!

I'm not walking in fear anymore. Paul and I have shared this journey and together we have watched Nicholas and Jonathon grow up and have been there for them every step of the way, cheering them on from the side lines and comforting them, loving them. Nicholas is now away at university studying architecture and Jonathon is about to leave to study art. He hopes to work in computer animation in the film industry one day.

They have been such a gift from God. My Father, for whom there is no substitute, no drug, no food. He is a God who is big enough to satisfy each of our needs, because He is the only God who stills the hunger of those He loves, now and always.

Ps.17:14-15: 'You *still the hunger* of those you cherish; their sons have plenty, and they store up wealth for their children.   And I — in righteousness I shall see your face; when I awake, I shall be satisfied with seeing your likeness.'

Jonathon

Nicholas

Acknowledgements

I **WISH TO THANK** the following who helped me along the first part of the road to recovery, for their faith, perseverance and patience: Ann and Ken Bothamley, Howard and Elizabeth Reece-Smith, Melita Cullis. Paul Fellowes, for playing his guitar and singing to me in hospital! Without you all, I couldn't have done it and I'm incredibly grateful to you because, having tried to do it myself, I know it wasn't easy!

Rev Jonathan Wilmot, for his encouragement and support of us as a family, for which I'm enormously thankful; Steve and Zoe Goss, for showing me how to renew my mind and encouraging me to believe in my identity as a child of God; Phil and Shirley Cole, for supporting us with the host family programme run with Greyfriars Church; Eileen Mitson, for believing in this book and reading and editing it countless times over; Rev Pads Dolphin, for his help with editing Chapter 9, originally the first chapter; Dr David McDonald, for listening and reading, with steadfast equanimity.

Whilst the hospital experiences described in this book have been met with astonishment by those who've read it, I have also had some exceptionally good doctors, to whom I'm extremely grateful and wish to express my thanks: Drs

Nick Longhurst, Maurice Robinson, David Clayton and Brian Matthews.

Thanks also to Will Gibson, for his great photography for the cover design (www.flickr.com/photos/wigiphotography/) and Anna Macky for patiently modelling for us – we had a great day out in Oxford with Nicholas leading the way until we found the perfect setting in one of the colleges. Lunch in the 'oldest pub in Oxford' went down very well!

My very dear and much loved friends, Alison, Rose, Amanda and Sarah, who've weaved in and out of my story from the beginning and each provided me with support in a variety of ways during those turbulent years.

I often wonder what I would have done without Paul, and whether all the hard work put in by others could have been sustained without him by my side. We've been through so much together. Paul, your resolute stability and tranquillity in the midst of chaos has been a breath of fresh air to me.

Nicholas and Jonathon, for whom my love knows no bounds.

I want to include here a final word from Joanie Yoder, taken from an email to me in August 2003. Joanie was my mentor as I began to write this book and she encouraged and supported me as we put the host family programme into practice. Sadly, Joanie died in October 2004 and I've missed her terribly, but praise God for her faith and example. Her faith lead to establishing Yeldall Manor, one of the most successful Christian rehabilitation centres for men in the UK. Her faith remains hugely inspirational.

'Pioneering for God means cutting a new path for the Lord, for yourselves and for others who will come after you, and opening up a new territory for good news and freedom. I think the words in Luke 3:4-6 describe this: 'Prepare the way for the Lord, make straight paths for him. Every valley shall be filled in, every mountain and hill made low. The crooked roads shall become straight, the rough ways smooth. And all mankind will see God's salvation.'

Such pioneering is costly, mainly because it means paying prices that few others would be prepared to pay. (how well I know this, and so do you!) But pioneers are willing to pay those prices because they know that the ministry they are pioneering is first and foremost God's vision. Therefore he is ultimately responsible for it. So they stay with the vision he's given and maintain it by faith, even when it appears to be dying. But once a ministry has been put on the map by its pioneers, God will raise up a growing number of people to go forward in it, and many sin-sick people 'will see the salvation of the Lord!'

Appendix

HERE ARE SOME of the typical lies common to many people, particularly to those suffering with eating disorders and self harm. What may appear irrational to some are not only believed by others, but also control their whole way of living.

These verses can be used as stronghold busters in the following format:

LIE: I am worthless.

TRUTH: A Christian is never worthless!

John 15:1-5: 'I am a branch of the true vine, Jesus, a channel of His life.'

Eph.2:10: 'For we are God's workmanship, created in Christ Jesus to do good works, which God prepared in advance for us to do.'

Prayer: Heavenly Father, I renounce the lie that I am worthless and I accept the truth that I am a branch of the true vine, Jesus, a channel of His life. I choose to believe that I have been created to do good works, which you have already prepared for me to do. Amen.

LIE: I am insignificant.

Jn.15:16:   'I have been chosen and appointed
                       by God to bear fruit.'

LIE: I am unloved.

Jn.16:27:   'The Father Himself loves me.'

LIE: If I were good enough/loved enough/clever
enough, what happened to me would not have happened.

Rom.8:35-39:   'I cannot be separated from the love
                       of God.'
Ps.139:16-18:   'All the days ordained for me were
                       written in your book before one of
                       them came to be. How precious to
                       me are your thoughts, O God! How
                       vast is the sum of them! Were I to
                       count them, they would outnumber
                       the grains of sand. When I awake, I
                       am still with you.'

LIE: I am useless.

2Tim.2:21:   'I will be used for special purposes
                       because I am dedicated and useful to
                       God.'

LIE: I am a failure.

Phil.4:13:   'I can do all things through Christ
                        who strengthens me.'

EATING DISORDERS:

LIE: Because I am a failure I need to succeed at losing
weight.

Eph.2:6:   'I am God's workmanship, created
                        for good works.'

Rom.8:6:   'Being controlled by the human
                        nature results in death and I am
                        controlled by the Spirit which
                        results in life and peace.'

LIE: I can control my feelings and circumstances by
controlling my food intake.

Rom.8:6:   'To be controlled by the Spirit
                        results in life and peace.'

LIE: I hate myself and my body.

1Cor.6:19:   'My body is the temple of the Holy
                        Spirit, given to me by God.

Ps.139:13-14:   'For you created my inmost being;
                        you knit me together in my mother's
                        womb. I praise you because I am
                        fearfully and wonderfully made.'

LIE: I need to punish myself by not allowing myself the pleasure of enjoying food.

Rom8:1:	'Therefore, there is now no condemnation for those who are in Christ Jesus.'
1Cor.12:27:	'I am a member of Christ's body.'
Mt.6:25:	'Life is worth more than food.'

LIE: If I eat I lose control which causes me extreme anxiety.

Rom.8:6:	'I am controlled by the Spirit which results in life and peace.'
1Pet.5:7:	'I can leave all my anxieties with God because He cares for me.'

LIE: I can only eat in secret because it is a failing to be seen eating.

Mt.6:25:	'Life is worth more than food.'
Phil.4:13:	'I can do all things through Christ who strengthens me.'

LIE: I cannot cope with the sensation of food within my stomach, which I find repulsive and uncomfortable.

1Cor.6:13:	'Food is for my stomach and my stomach is for food.'

LIE: I can avoid all stressful situations by being anorectic.

1Pet.5:7:   'I can leave all my worries with God because He cares for me.'

LIE: I would rather die than gain weight.

Mt.6:25:   'Life is worth more than food.'
Ps.139:13-14:   'For you created my inmost being; you knit me together in my mother's womb. I praise you because I am fearfully and wonderfully made.'

LIE: If I eat I will get fat and be repulsive and more unloved.

Mt.6:25:   'Life is worth more than food.'
Col.2:10:   'I am complete in Christ.'
Jn.14:21:   'He who loves me will be loved by my Father, and I too will love him and show myself to him.'

LIE: I feel better and more in control when I lose weight.

Rom.8:6:   'Being controlled by human nature results in death; I am controlled by the Spirit which results in life and peace.'

LIE: The thinner I can be, the more in control I will be.

Rom.8:6:   'Being controlled by human nature
                     results in death; I am controlled by
                     the Spirit which results in life and
                     peace.'

LIE: To lose weight and die of starvation is the ultimate
goal I can achieve.

Phil.3:14:   'The ultimate goal is to receive the
                     prize of God's call through Christ
                     Jesus.'

LIE: I will always be anorectic.

2Tim.1:7:   'I have not been given a spirit of
                     fear but of power, love and a sound
                     mind.'

LIE: It is easier to remain anorectic than to make any
steps forward.

Eph.3:20:   'God's power working in me is able
                     to do so much more than I can ever
                     ask for or even think of.'

LIE: This is too big for me to deal with and I need somebody else to take it away.

Phil.4:13:   'I can do all things through Christ who strengthens me.'

LIE: I am nothing.

1Cor.3:16:   'I am a temple of God.'

LIE: I am abandoned and rejected.

Phil.3:20:   'I am a citizen of heaven.'
Rom.8:35-39:   'I cannot be separated from the love of God.'

LIE: I cannot go on, I want to die.

Phil.4:13:   'I can do all things through Christ who strengthens me.'
Jn.3:16:   'I believe in Jesus so I may not die but have eternal life.'

LIE: I need to vomit if I eat because I cannot cope with food inside my body.

1Cor.6:13:   'Food is for my stomach and my stomach is for food.'

LIE: When I binge I lose control and it feels like I am being controlled by an outside force.

Rom.8:6:   'I am controlled by the Spirit which results in life and peace.'

SELF HARM

LIE: I can only feel loved by being ill, through receiving treatment and care from others.

Rom.8:35-39:   'I cannot be separated from the love of God.'
Is.66:13   'As a mother comforts her child, so will I comfort you; and you will be comforted.'

LIE: I need to punish myself if I eat, by other methods of self-harm, such as laxatives and cutting myself.

Lev.19:28:   'Do not cut your bodies...or put tattoo marks on yourselves.'
1Cor.12:27:   'I am a member of Christ's body.'
Mt.6:25:   'Life is worth more than food.'

LIE: I feel relief from my suffering when I cut myself.

Jer.16:1-7:   'The Lord says no one will cut themselves to show their grief.'

References

Freedom in Christ Ministries UK

Steps to Freedom in Christ
Living Free in Christ Discipleship Course by Neil Anderson and Steve Goss, both published by Monarch. These can be ordered via the Freedom in Christ website, www.ficm.org.uk where you will also find other valuable resources for your church.

Finding the God-Dependent Life: A Personal Story of a Life Transformed by the Secret of 'God Dependence' over Co-Dependence by Joanie Yoder, published by Discovery House (May 1992)

God Alone: Heartfelt Encouragement from the Pages of Our Daily Bread by Joanie Yoder, published by Discovery House (Sept 2006)

The Hiding Place by Corrie Ten Boom, published by Hodder & Stoughton (18 Nov 2004)

Bringing Heaven in to Hell by Merlin R Carothers, published by Kingsway Publications; New edition (21 Jan 1994)

Yeldall Manor, Wargrave, Berkshire.
Yeldall Manor provides Christian rehabilitation for men with drug and alcohol addictions.
www.yeldall.org.uk

Still the Hunger

Still the Hunger exists to support those with mental health needs. For more information please visit our website at:
www.stillthehunger.co.uk

Please note that a large number of names and places in this book have been changed for confidentiality reasons.

About the Author

B everley lives in Reading, Berkshire with her husband Paul and two sons, Nicholas and Jonathon. She is part of the Freedom in Christ teaching team and has a particular interest in helping people overcome negative patterns of irrational thinking and emotional behaviour disturbance through the process of renewing the mind. Beverley ran her own wedding cake business during the 1990's. She worked as a senior manager within the NHS before setting up Still the Hunger to provide support for those with mental health needs.

For more information on Still the Hunger please visit our website: www.stillthehunger.co.uk